Living Fully, Dying Well

by Rueben Job

Abingdon Press

09 10 11 12 13 — 8 7 6 5

Table of Contents

Introduction. 4

1. Living Fully 9

2. A Theology of Aging 18

3. Our Culture's View of Aging 27

4. Finding Purpose and Meaning in Life. 33

5. Getting It All Together: Making Decisions . . 42

6. Dying Well 54

7. What Happens When We Die? 62

8. How Then Shall We Live? 76

Acknowledgments

This resource began many years ago in a seminar on Spirituality and Aging. As I listened to participants respond to the subject it became clear that there was regret at not having claimed the inheritance that belongs to all who love and seek to follow the way of God, and there was disappointment that the Church had not provided more help in preparing young and old to face death. For more than a decade this issue has been opening the door of my awareness and demanding attention.

While the issue has been claiming my attention, it was Belmont United Methodist Church, Edgehill United Methodist Church, and their GOLD (Gift of Life Discoveries) Task Force that made the project a priority. Members of the Task Force, interested friends, the senior pastor, and my own life experience seemed to declare that this was the time to begin a new conversation about living fully and dying well. The United Methodist Publishing House, and especially Susan Salley, Executive Director of Church Program Resources, offered encouragement, direction, and editorial skill to transform the various pieces of the resource into an integrated, accessible, and useful whole. I offer my deep gratitude to those listed above and to the many persons who have helped me to understand more completely what it means to live fully and to die well.

Introduction

Living fully is life's most rewarding gift. Young or old, rich or poor, at the peak of our performance or at low ebb of our vitality, life remains a precious gift and we may savor its richness throughout our lifetime.

Often the awareness of this precious gift is overshadowed by our busy, almost frenetic activities. The gospels encourage us to be good stewards of this gift but also to take time to reflect on its beauty, meaning, goodness, and eternal nature. Preparation for this kind of abundant, joyful, and fulfilling living is not possible without thoughtful consideration of life's ending.

Our culture often denies the reality of death and usually views death as a negative experience. The gospels, while recognizing the pain of separation brought on by death, nevertheless see life as a whole and death as a transition from life in the reign of God not fully realized to life in God's full reign in heaven.

In the past five years, I have had the privilege of being close at hand as first my sister-in-law, then my oldest brother, and more recently, my second and last brother faced the experience of dying. I call it a privilege because each shared openly about their fears and their faith as they experienced what can only be described as a good death. Each of them had lived a full life and had made more preparation than most for this last great experience of life.

In each case they were surrounded by those who loved them, by skilled medical professionals, loving caregivers, and the gentle and wise care provided by hospice staff.

Not all die full of years and ready to embrace this last experience of life, largely perhaps because we are unprepared for death whether it comes soon or late. It would be foolish to say that the death of a child, a young mother, or an aging grandfather each have the same impact or consequence for those who remain. Yet when we take seriously the gospel teaching that life is eternal, death does indeed lose its sting.

All of us will die and all of us think about death. But remarkably we seldom talk about death in a calm and rational way. The emphasis of our culture is on youth and staying young, and even the church has been strangely silent about one of the two most universal experiences of all humans, birth and death.

Why the silence? Is it because this greatest mystery is something we do not understand? Is it because we fear the end of life as we know it and therefore deny the reality of death? Is it because we simply do not have the will to face our own mortality? Is it because we do not want to be considered "otherworldly," disconnected from the real issues of life in the here and now?

Is it because our theology has no place for life that is eternal? Jesus had a lot to say about the eternal nature of life, and he lived a life that demonstrated an awareness of living at home in the kingdom of God in both this world and the next. Why is the church so hesitant to share this way of living? Could it be that we do not know how to keep these two homes in balance? Living at home with God in this world and trusting that we will live at home with God in the world to come is not as easy as it may seem in a society that is in denial about the active presence of God in this world and the promise of the world to come.

To live fully and die well requires deep personal faith as well as an inviting, vital, welcoming, supportive, and nurturing community of faith that presents opportunities to talk openly, honestly, and frequently about the mystery of this last great experience of life in this world. This material seeks to make possible that kind of honest and faithful seeking that guides us to discoveries about ourselves, leads us to a new level of joyful living each day, and helps us make the kind of careful preparations that will offer the opportunity of dying well when our days in this world are coming to an end.

Our life is not without purpose. No matter who or where you are, your life has meaning. You can make a difference for good in the world. We do have a destination, and all of life is indeed a journey that for the Christian leads toward God in this life and the life to come. Christians through the centuries have proclaimed that death is the doorway that brings us finally and fully home to God and to the place where all the saints are gathered in light and life.

The good news is that we do not make this journey alone. Our faithful Savior has promised to send another One to teach us, companion us, guide us, and stand beside us in all of life's experience (John 14:16). With God's help through the power of the Holy Spirit, we are able to live fully every day and embrace with trust, obedience, and hope the day of our transition from life in this world to life in the next.

Rueben P. Job
Autumn 2006

Living Fully

Living fully every day means living in the confidence and joy that God loves each one of us completely, without qualification, and extravagantly, as a parent loves a child. How can we as Christians claim this good news and this inheritance to live every day in God's presence?

Scripture

...so that, with the eyes of your heart enlightened, you may know what is the hope to which he has called you, what are the riches of his glorious inheritance among the saints, and what is the immeasurable greatness of his power for us who believe.... .

Ephesians 1:18-19

Prayer

Giver and Sustainer of life, we give you thanks for the good and precious gift of life we have been given. Teach us how to be good stewards of the inheritance we have in Christ, and grant us wisdom and guidance so that we may live fully and faithfully every day. We are yours and seek to live as your children this day and always. Amen.

I think all of us want to live the good life. We want to live a life that is rich, honorable, enjoyable, and faithful, a life that leaves the world a better place than we found it. We want to live life fully, and when our time comes we want to die well. And for each of us that kind of living and that kind of dying means something unique, because each of us is unique.

There are some things that are universally true of a good life and a good death. In this chapter, we are going to focus on a couple of the essential elements or characteristics of the foundation of the good life for those of us who seek to live as disciples of Jesus. What are those qualities and characteristics of living that each one of us wants to claim for ourselves and for those we love? What are those qualities and characteristics that transcend everything that has happened or may happen to us in our daily lives?

Take a moment of silence and think about what you would need in your life to be able to say that you are living fully.

From Youth to Maturity

In youth we know the joy and delight of peak experiences, but we may not have learned how important and precious every moment of life really is. When we are young we may experience life in depth, but we have meager standards against which to measure that experience and the value of every moment of life.

As we mature we begin to place a higher value on the gift of life, recognizing that, young or old, there is no guarantee about tomorrow. And we begin to realize it when we become aware of our own process of aging and discover, as the Bible says, that we are "full of years." If we are fortunate, we gradually learn to savor the moment rather than wishing it away for some unknown tomorrow.

As we age we also begin to realize that our remaining lifetime is short, and we begin to appreciate every moment of living as precious and sacred. Time with those we love, time in worship or study and reflection, attention to our avocation, or things left undone suddenly become more important as the awareness builds that life in this world is limited. No matter how well we take care of our bodies, our lives cannot be extended without limit. No matter how many vitamins we take, surgeries and transplants we undergo, life as we know it in this world will end.

Claiming our Inheritance

As children of God we are in line for a great inheritance, the sign of which is evident in the celebration of our birth and in our baptism. But what are the particulars of this inheritance and how do we claim it every day of our lives?

Even as we age we may miss seeing, appropriating, and enjoying our full inheritance as children of God. We may have spent many years going to church, reading the Bible, and praying, and still not be in touch with the promised inheritance to those who love, trust, obey, and seek God with their entire being.

While the good news of the gospel is so amazing it should fill us with joy and hope every day, we sometimes neglect to take the time to reflect upon and incorporate that good news into our daily living.

If someone were to leave us with a huge inheritance—more money than we could possibly spend and property scattered throughout the world—and we were to ignore it, people would think us a bit strange. Our inheritance—our confidence in God's extravagant love for us and presence in our lives—is waiting for us. It would seem strange to leave this huge inheritance hidden and dormant when it could be invested wisely and result in a more joyful, peaceful, rich, faithful, and fruitful life.

The early Church was often as distracted from the central truth of the gospel as are we. That may be why when we dip into almost any book or chapter of the New Testament, we find another jewel of our inheritance. They, as we, needed to be reminded about who they were and what kind of life they were being offered as children of God.

The author of Ephesians uses extravagant language to document this enormous inheritance that belongs to every Christian:

Blessed be the God and Father of our Lord Jesus Christ, who has blessed us in Christ with every spiritual blessing... just as he chose us in Christ before the foundation of the world to be holy and blameless before him in love.... In him we have redemption through his blood, the forgiveness of our trespasses, according to the riches of his grace that he lavished on us. (Ephesians 1:3-4, 7)

As followers of Jesus Christ we claim this blessing for ourselves. This love was not some afterthought; according to Ephesians, this Creator God chose us to receive this lavish love even before the earth was formed. However, most of us would confess that it is difficult for us to think of ourselves as being chosen by God before the creation of the world and even more difficult to think of ourselves as blameless before God.

How can we overlook the testimony of Paul in the eighth chapter of Romans when he says, "If God is for us, who is against us?... I am convinced that neither death, nor life, nor angels, nor rulers, nor things present, nor things to come, nor powers, nor height, nor depth, nor anything else in all creation, will be able to separate us from the love of God in Christ Jesus our Lord" (Romans 8:31, 38-39).

Here is yet another text that speaks clearly about our inheritance as children of God. Nothing, absolutely nothing, can separate us from the love of God. To remember that we are held secure in the love of God in every circumstance is to take a giant step toward claiming our inheritance for ourselves.

Think for a moment how would you feel if you discovered that you had an inheritance of half a billion dollars. Would you pay attention to it? What difference would it make in your life? What would you do? The discovery would probably shake up your whole life. Daily routines, concerns, activities, and thoughts would be changed.

You may not inherit a great sum of money, but you do have an inheritance waiting for you as God's child. What would change if you suddenly discovered and took to heart the gospel, the good news about God's love and care for you? Would it change the way you think about yourself, about the world? Would it banish your fears and give you a new freedom to live fully and joyfully?

While our inheritance as children of God is beyond our full comprehension, there are some elements of that inheritance that stand out in sharp relief in the Scriptures. The first of these, of course, is God's love for all creation and specifically for humankind.

Roberta Bondi, a highly acclaimed writer and seminary professor, put it this way in her book, *In Ordinary Time*:

> Before anything else, above all else, beyond everything else, God loves us. God loves us extravagantly, ridiculously, without limit or condition. God is in love with us. God is besotted with us. God yearns for us. God does not love us "in spite of who we are" or "for whom God knows we can become." According to the wonderful fourth- and fifth-century teachers I have learned from and also teach myself, God loves us hopelessly as mothers love their babies.... God loves us, the very people we are; and not only that, but, even against what we ourselves sometimes find plausible, God likes us. (Abingdon Press, 2001)

Now isn't that good news? Can you imagine anyone ignoring or discarding this part of our inheritance? Living my days out of such knowledge changes everything. What do I have to fear about the imperfections of my own life that need to move toward perfection, when I know that I dwell in the loving presence of the One who alone can make me more than I am? The Creator of all that exists loves me and likes me just as I am.

What disappointment can dampen my deep peace and abiding joy when I know I am the object of this great love that will never leave, forsake, condemn, or fail? What challenge can overcome and strike fear in my heart when I remember who it is that loves me, provides for me, sustains me, guides and keeps me? It is in this unqualified and unlimited love that we find confidence and hope for daily life.

Light in a Violent World

Threats of a violent and uncertain world lose their power when we live out of this knowledge that God loves us as though we were the sole object of that love, and that God loves all creation with that same intensity and unqualified love.

Of course, there is plenty to be concerned about and much that needs our prayerful and vigorous attention in the world. These days we could be overwhelmed by the lust for power that seems to have plunged our entire nation into the mud bath of corruption. We could try to forget the starving children of the world crying out for food and shelter as a select few on God's good earth hoard resources for themselves. We could be tempted to turn away in fear from the needs of the world. But when we are clear about our inheritance as children of God we also become clear that all of God's children are the objects of God's seeking and saving love. That is why we are called to do our part to leave this world a better, safer, more equitable place than we found it.

As the truth of the gospel begins to take root in our hearts and minds, we realize that the ultimate goal of this incredible saving love will be fulfilled. As Romans declares, "...the creation itself will be set free from its bondage to decay and will obtain the freedom of the glory of the children of God" (Romans 8:21). The darkness of evil, violence, and disaster cannot put out the light of God's all-excelling love in our individual lives or in the entire creation.

Personal Fears and Loss

Even the darkness of our own doubts and fears and the fractured and warring world cannot overcome the light of God's amazing love. It was Jesus who said, "I am the way, and the truth, and the life" (John 14:6). And John said of Jesus, "In the beginning was the Word. ...in him was... the light of all people. The light shines in the darkness, and the darkness did not overcome it." (John 1:1, 4-5)

Will there be disappointments, pain, loss, disease, and death itself? Of course. We are not promised and we should not expect to be spared from the challenges and limitations of life any more than we should relinquish the opportunities, rewards, and gifts that life offers.

God's love is surely our greatest inheritance, for when we remember that each one of us is embraced in that incomprehensible and unqualified love, we realize that regardless of our circumstances, we have all we can ever need.

And if there is but one part of your inheritance that you remember, let it be this: you are God's beloved, just as you are, now, this very moment and for all time. Write it on a card and place it on the mirror where you will see it every day. Write it on your heart. Remember who you are!

Because of that great love for us, God offers other gifts as well. One of the greatest is the gift of God's abiding presence with us. It was the resurrected Christ who declared, "... I am with you always, to the end of the age" (Matthew 28:20). And here is another witness from the book of Hebrews: "... for he has said, 'I will never leave you or forsake you.' So we can say with confidence, 'The Lord is my helper; I will not be afraid. What can anyone do to me?'" (Hebrews 13:5-6).

These are some of the Biblical texts that declare the nearly incomprehensible nature of our inheritance as children of God. The love, mercy, and capacity to care for those who give themselves to God and God's way are made clear in the Scriptures. Our inheritance as children of God is centered in God's character and love and is never determined by our achievements or failures.

Our Constant Companion

Whether we are at the peak of our powers or nearing the point of despair, it is important to remember who we are as children of this loving God, a God made known in countless ways but most clearly revealed in the life, death, and resurrection of Jesus. It is this God who has given us life, loves us, sustains us, accompanies us, and promises never to leave us. It is this God who is capable of guiding us and sustaining us through all of life.

Most of us have at times felt alone and wondered if God was really absent from our lives and our world, or if we were somehow unable to perceive divine presence with us and within us.

We all face difficult decisions and unknown territory as we age. But we do not face those decisions and that unknown territory alone. There is One who comes alongside to help us, guide us, assist us, comfort us, and bring us safely home to God.

Consequently, we can walk with confidence and courage even when we face the most lonely and the most dark and difficult experiences of life. For even there, this God of light and love embraces us, holds us close, and is with us to guide, comfort, and sustain.

It is this promise and the accumulated experience of the saints who have gone before that gives encouragement to us as we seek to be faithful in trusting and obeying this God of love.

We are therefore aware that we are never alone, need never be caught in the grips of fear, never crushed by the burden of guilt, and never overcome with anxiety about the future.

Do you struggle with fully realizing God's love for you?

Even if one of us should forget this truth for a moment, we can remind each other that we belong to this mighty God of love who will never forsake us and promises to always be with us to guide us, comfort us, enable us, and lead us each and all home to the promised land prepared by God that even now awaits our arrival.

Resources

In Ordinary Time, by Roberta C. Bondi (Abingdon Press, 2001).

What are Old People For?, by William H. Thomas (VanderWyk & Burnham, 2004).

Honoring African American Elders, by Anne Streaty Wimberly, editor (Jossey-Bass, 1997).

Reflections on Aging and Spiritual Growth, by Andrew J. Weaver, Harold George Koenig, Phyllis C. Roe, editors (Abingdon, 1998).

2 A Theology of Aging

Age doesn't preclude a new call to purpose and hope. God is with us, going ahead of us to prepare the way, at every stage in our lives.

Scripture

...in all things we are more than conquerors through him who loved us. For I am convinced that neither death, nor life, nor angels, nor rulers, nor things present, nor things to come, nor powers, nor height, nor depth, nor anything else in all creation, will be able to separate us from the love of God in Christ Jesus our Lord.   Romans 8:37-39

Prayer

Creator God, we thank you for the gift of life that you have given to each of us, and we thank you for sustaining us all the days of our lives and for bringing us to this time together. We invite and welcome your presence in our midst and ask that you will guide our minds and hearts as we seek to know you and follow you more faithfully. Thank you for hearing our prayers and accepting our lives as we offer them to you in the name and spirit of Jesus Christ. Amen.

Aging happens whether we want it to or not. The culture around us tries to convince us that we can avoid the aging process, but our own bodies betray that notion day after day. We encourage everyone to live wisely and choose a healthy lifestyle because it adds so much to the quality of the lives we live. And with wholesome living and good genes, we may indeed live much, much longer than the average life span of our day. But the reality does not change; aging happens whether we want it to or not.

I wasn't ready to receive my AARP membership invitation in the mail after turning fifty. I didn't ask for it, but they surprised me anyway. I realized that this well-known organization was extending its membership recruitment efforts to a younger demographic, but I was also reminded that I had "crossed over." I had moved into the latter stages of middle adulthood and was not too many years away from a new classification often referred to as elders or seniors.

The fact that I was aging was not an entirely new thought. I had already experienced a number of noticeable changes. My rate of metabolism had slowed and now I had to watch my weight more rigorously. Age spots appeared, I did not have the stamina I once had, and being prematurely gray I was once asked if my sixteen-year-old son was my grandson. I knew I was aging and that some of the goals of life would not be realized. But I still wasn't ready to be a member of AARP.

Reality of Aging: Benefits and Challenges

As we grow older we do notice that our capacities change, and we experience many forms of diminishment. What once was easy becomes a test of will and endurance as our bodies age and become less flexible and we begin to lose some of the strength of young muscle and bone. Aches and pains that seldom made their way into our consciousness can now become constant and annoying companions. Arms become too short to hold reading material at a distance at which it can be easily read, and adequate lighting, while necessary and good, is not enough to overcome diminished vision.

The reality of aging captures our attention when we realize that time is flowing on and with each passing moment our time on earth grows shorter, noticeably shorter. In our youth the end of life seems so far away, and in our mid-years we are so often preoccupied with career and family that we pay little attention to that way-off horizon that marks the end of life in this world. However, as we move into our elder years we become increasingly aware that every life has limits and that our time on earth is finite.

While this is an honest assessment and an essential review for our well-being and our planning for the future, it is not the entire picture. Yes, there is less time, and there is diminishment of capacities, but there is more to the story. And that more is often hidden away and neglected, as is the honest look at the diminishment of aging. We do lose some capacities as we age, but we also augment others and may even discover some we never knew existed. The Bible reminds us, "Even though our outer nature is wasting away, our inner nature is being renewed day by day" (2 Corinthians 4:16). If we are granted the gift of long life we are certain to experience the limitations of aging, but we may also experience the benefits of aging, including a deeper understanding of the meaning of life, the rewards of rich memories, deep gratitude for the gift of life itself, opportunities to invest ourselves in making the world a better place, and last but not least, the renewal of our deepest inner spiritual life.

Perhaps it is the larger amount of time we can dedicate to thinking, reflecting, reading, praying, and serving that begins to incubate new patterns of living, new ways of thinking, and new ways of using the gifts God has placed in our lives. Whatever the reason, we have all heard stories of persons who late in life made enormous discoveries, created inventions, painted wonderful works of art, wrote books that changed the world, and found incredible fulfillment in serving others. You may be listed in that group now, some time soon, or in the distant future. However, each of us can learn to more fully appreciate the gift of each day and learn to be a better steward of the gift of life as long as we live. Every age group can make the world a better place to live and enjoy the rewards of living fully as a child of God every day.

God in All Stages of Life

I believe God is deeply involved in every stage of life and that our life with and in God is an indispensable resource for every stage of life. No more important in the latter stage than before, but perhaps we are more open to receiving and utilizing this resource that was there all the time but that we were too preoccupied to notice.

Yes, aging happens whether we want it to or not. But the good news is that in the Christian view all of life is a gift from God, and is always and at all times lived in God's presence and with God's companionship to guide and sustain us. The story of our faith reminds us that God is always calling us forth into the future. Abraham and Sarah are primary examples of elders who received the call to go into the future with a promise that their faithful journey would be rewarded. In their senior years, God called Abraham and Sarah to leave their home to enter a new and uncertain future, one that brought a new family, a new home, and a lasting covenant (Genesis 17).

As with Abraham and Sarah, our own life may best be seen as pilgrimage, a journey with God and toward God's desirable future. Life is framed for us in terms of a sense of past and a sense of future. The future is often formatted for us by horizons near and far. While we do not see beyond the far horizon, we

do know who inhabits the horizon, near or far.
Consequently, we speak confidently about our plans to
complete a project, see our grandchildren, take an extended
trip, enjoy retirement, and attend numerous celebrations of
life's milestones.

Looking Ahead

We seem to be happiest, most productive, and most
teachable when we are looking forward to something.
Looking forward implies a positive future and seems to be
necessary for our sense of well-being. We could refer to
this need to look forward as a horizon of consciousness.
Our horizons of consciousness change with the passing of
time. When we are young the future seems to stretch out
indefinitely, and even next week seems like a long time in
the distance. When we are children we are conscious of the
horizon of going to high school. When we are in high
school we look forward to college or career. Our young
adult years often focus on career, marriage, and family. The
middle adult years bring plans for retirement and an
assessment of things left to accomplish. But always a
meaningful and positive horizon is needed for us to be
fulfilled and happy.

Aging inevitably changes things. As we get older and
experience diminishment of our physical capacities we can
easily become captive to discouragement and even
depression. But it need not be so. While diminishment often
accompanies aging, there is also the opportunity of
expanded opportunities that escaped our notice in younger
years.

The God in whom we place our lives and our trust is the
One who is never finished with us. God is with us in every
moment of our existence and is always providing new
possibilities for abundant living. In the shortened time

remaining, God gives us opportunity to discover the deeper wisdom and the most important things about life. With the diminishment of physical capacities God invites the enhancement of our spiritual sensibilities through prayer, reflection, lifelong learning, sharing wisdom, caring for relationship, and offering encouragement and assistance for good and worthy causes.

Abundant and Eternal Life

We celebrate the birth of each child with rich and meaningful liturgy, but we sometimes miss the celebration of life that is abundant and eternal in a liturgy of death and resurrection. Our faith literally shouts that there is more than a diminishing physical capacity to aging. The God in whom we place our faith and trust is the One who never lets us go, is never finished with our formation and transformation, and will never leave us helpless and alone. It is in God that we find our hope for every age and every circumstance of life. As we move toward our final horizon with God we can do so with confidence and even anticipation. In faith our dying becomes another opening to God, whose horizons are without end. With God we always have something to look forward to.

This is true because the God in whom we place our trust is a particular God who is made known in sacred text, the magnificent creation, the events of history, the words of prophet and priest, and most clearly in the life of Jesus Christ. Belief in God may be nearly a universal human characteristic. But for Christians God is seen and understood most clearly in the life, death, and resurrection of Jesus Christ. The incarnation brings dramatic and new revelation into the mystery, character, will, and love of God.

God is seen in new ways in the life of Jesus of Nazareth. We no longer think of God as some distant, disinterested, and disengaged power. Now we see God with a face and heart we can understand, the face and heart of Jesus. In Jesus we see a God who can be known and whose invitation to faithful companionship in life that is abundant and eternal can be trusted. In Jesus we see a God who knows our doubts and faith, our fears and confidence, and who hears and understands our prayers.

Jesus defines God for us and he did for those first disciples who walked, ate, slept, and prayed with him along the shores of Galilee. It was from his words and his life that those first disciples learned that God was like a loving Abba. God was experienced as a loving parent whose will and purpose always sought good for all. God was experienced as One who cared for and provided for all creation.

Because God is infinite and each one of us is unique, we have our own distinct image or picture of who God is and how God relates to us and invites our response. For the Christian this picture is always seen most clearly in Jesus Christ. All of us can learn from him to face the reality of the limits of our mortal life and embrace the unlimited nature of life abundant and eternal that Jesus taught and promised for all who followed him.

Living with the Gospels, the Epistles, and the Book of Acts we get a new understanding of God's love and God's grace. There are various stories and texts that paint the picture of God for us as we seek to know and love the One who knows and loves us beyond measure. A passage that many carry in their heart is found in the eighth chapter of Romans: "…in all these things we are more than conquerors through him who loved us. For I am convinced that neither death, nor life, nor angels, nor rulers, nor things present, nor things to come, nor powers, nor height, nor depth, nor anything else in all creation, will be able to separate us from the love of God in Christ Jesus our Lord" (Romans 8:37-39).

A Photographer's Perspective

As we age we begin to see that the horizon of life is not unlimited, and the weeks seem to fly by ever more rapidly. When we move into our senior years we suddenly discover that the years seem to fly by faster than the weeks did in our youth. And it is now that we begin to look more honestly at that final horizon that awaits every person. We have often been silent and timid about considering the final act of life in this world. And as other chapters will point out, our culture is in deep denial about aging and death. Because this cultural view is so prevalent we can be easily carried along with this great deception and miss the richness of every stage of life. This resource is one effort to help us live more fully every day and one day experience a good death as we claim our full inheritance as children of God.

The effect of moving closer to our final horizon with God might be compared to a photographic metaphor of changing from a wide-angle camera lens to a telephoto or zoom lens. A wide-angle lens spans far from side to side and includes objects in the foreground and those that are in the far distance. A telephoto lens, on the other hand, "pulls" us in closer and tighter to a particular object. As our view gets closer and tighter, our focus shifts from the general things on the sides, in the foreground, and in the irrelevant distance to the object of our immediate concern. By analogy, viewing life in our middle years might be like looking through a wide-angle lens: we see lots of things all around us and even in the distant future. But as we are drawn closer to life's final horizon, our view becomes more closely and tightly focused. We don't need to see a lot of things, only those that matter most. As we draw closer to life's final horizon we want to see God as that welcoming and gracious reality that is always on our side. This final move is what Paul spoke of in his finest treatise on love as the most important of all realities: "For now we see in a mirror, dimly, but then we will see face to face. Now I know only in part; then I will know fully, even as I have been fully known" (1 Corinthians 13:12).

As our final horizon in this life draws near, we often discover a deeper wisdom, a greater peace, and a fuller joy in each day we live. As we practice a lifetime of seeking to live in God's presence the final horizon of life in this world holds no dark shadows but rather a continuing invitation to move into the light and love of God's presence. Living with God means we always have something to look forward to, and even the great mystery of death and the transition from this life to the next can be faced honestly and with anticipation of an even fuller measure of the joy and fulfillment of living in God's presence that we now enjoy.

Resources

General Board of Discipleship, Center on Aging & Older Adult Ministries (*www.gbod.org/coa/mission.asp*)

International Longevity Center, A Center for Policy, Research & Education on Population Aging (*www.ilcusa.org*)

American Association of Retired Persons (*www.aarp.org*)

Aging Today: The Bimonthly Newspaper for the American Society on Aging (*www.agingtoday.org*)

Ten Gospel Promises for Later Life, by Jane Marie Thibault (Upper Room Books, 2005).

Have the Time of Your Life: Living for God in Each Moment, by Michael Long (Chalice Press, 2003).

Practicing our Faith, by Dorothy C. Bass, Editor (Jossey-Bass, 1997).

Our Culture's View of Aging

Our culture can present growing older in a negative way. How can we embrace the gifts of clarity, wisdom, and experience that aging brings?

Scripture

Listen to me, O house of Jacob, all the remnant of the house of Israel, who have been borne by me from your birth, carried from the womb; even to your old age I am he, even when you turn gray I will carry you.   Isaiah 46:3-4a

Prayer

Loving God, we thank you for the gift of life and for your sustaining grace that has cared for us and brought us to this moment. Teach us how to value every age and stage of life so that we may live fully every day, and one day, secure in your loving embrace, die a good death. We offer our prayers to you in the name and spirit of Christ. Amen.

When we pick up a daily newspaper or magazine, we are likely to see headlines calling attention to the growing older population in the United States. For example, the cover story of the November/December 2003 issue of *AARP Magazine* declared, "Sixty is the New Thirty." Even more recent, the cover of the August 30, 2004, issue of *Time* magazine read, "How to Live to Be 100 (And Not Regret It)." Such examples are testimony to the increasing numbers of older adults and the reality that aging is changing in America.

When Jesus was born some 2,000 years ago, average life expectancy was only about 22 years. When John Wesley was born in the eighteenth century, life expectancy at birth was around 35 years. As recently as one hundred years ago in the United States, life expectancy was 47 years. Today the figure is closer to 77 years. Some scientists predict that in the not too distant future people will enjoy a life expectancy of 120 years.

As a result of better health care, nutrition, job safety, physical fitness, scientific advances, medical technology, and a host of other variables, more people are living longer. Yet it is clear that we live in a society that is both age denying and age defying. The effort to enhance the quality of life for older adults continues to reap significant benefits. These efforts permit older adults to extend their years of life, enjoy life more, and make a larger contribution to society.

How Old Is Old?

Perhaps you are wondering when exactly a person becomes an older adult? The answer depends on a number of factors. To a four-year-old, a twelve-year-old sibling is "old"; to a thirteen-year-old, one's parents may not simply be old, but possibly ancient. To a forty-year-old someone nearing retirement is old; to a centenarian, however, an eighty-year-old person may be "young." Each of us has a notion, based on our own age at a particular point of time, about the meaning of the words old or young.

One denomination's Older Adult Ministries department suggests the following categories of aging for older adults: 55–74, young old age; 75–85, middle old age; and 86–100, old old age. We may feel that the categories do not fit us or our experience, but we probably all agree that the definition of older adult is rapidly changing.

In American society, we usually define old age as beginning at age sixty-five. Yet, nothing magical happens when we celebrate our sixty-fifth birthday. We do not turn old overnight. Aging is a lifelong process. Perhaps a good definition is something I recently read: "When your mind seeks what your body cannot fulfill, you're an older adult."

The Gifts of Age

Simone de Beauvoir, in *Coming of Age*, tells the story of a legend in a remote mountain village of Bali:

> In Bali it is said that once upon a time the people of a remote mountain village used to sacrifice, kill, and eat their old men. A day came when there was not a single old man left, and the traditions were lost. The tribal leaders wanted to build a great house for the meetings of the assembly, but when they came to look at the tree-trunks that had been cut for that purpose no one could tell the top from the bottom: if the timber were placed the wrong way up, it would set off a series of disasters. A young man came forward and stood before the village leaders. He said that if the villagers promised never to eat old men any more, he would be able to find a solution. The villagers promised. He brought his grandfather, whom he had hidden, and the old man taught the community to tell top from bottom. (Putnum, 1972)

The moral of this story is quite simple: neither our society nor our church can afford to have the faith, the experience, and the wisdom that often abounds in older adults be lost or underutilized. Our culture has not done well in recognizing and preserving the wisdom of its elders. Unfortunately, the church has not done much better. One of the challenges facing culture and church is to preserve and wisely invest the wisdom and skills of its elders, while preserving their dignity and providing a safe and secure place for them.

Perhaps this is a good time to reflect on the value you place on the experience, skill, and wisdom of older adults. From your perspective, do older adults get proper recognition, or too much or too little recognition? Do you see any need for change in our society's culture of aging? Does your congregation share your view of aging, that of our culture, or another view? Do you see the need for change, and if so, how can that best be accomplished and what do you need to do to bring about such desired change?

In the past, when people thought about growing older, they were more influenced by negative stereotypes of aging and focused on disease and disability of older adults. Our culture has viewed aging as descent: a process of deterioration and decline. This contributed to our negative views of aging and denial of the reality of aging. In denying aging, people didn't prepare for it. But with the changing image of what is possible as we age, we have a growing sense that we can do something to help make our aging a better and more positive experience. And, as Christians, our faith offers a vision of aging as a gift of God. Old age is not a burden but a gift that offers wonderful opportunities of learning, growing, sharing, experiencing, and mentoring.

Since many of us will live longer and healthier lives than previous generations did, we have the chance to create a second half of life that is very different from what our parents and grandparents experienced. We need not deny our aging but rather gain a new perspective of what it means to be persons of great worth as children of God.

Finding Meaning and Purpose

Our attitude about aging can be a great roadblock to our spiritual growth. But if we read the first book of the Bible carefully, we soon discover that Genesis offers the reader a spiritual identity that transcends age. When God first called Abraham he was getting on in years. God instructed him to leave Haran and to take his family and his possessions and venture forth at God's leading (Genesis 12:4). Abraham and Sarah were not young. Yet God told them to go forth so that they may be a light for all the nations. And, with God's help, this older couple began a new journey. In and through this journey, their life took on new meaning and purpose.

As we experience the second half of life as older adults, we too are invited to discover new meaning and purpose in living. Are we ever too young or too old to dream new dreams, or to invest our lives more fully? Not in the Biblical view of life. The truth is that we are invited to make a difference in our world just as Abraham and Sarah were invited to make a difference in theirs. We, as they, are invited to age with dignity, grace, and faith. In order to do that we will need to consider and cultivate the following:

- ◆ Embrace change
- ◆ Enjoy the freedom of growing older
- ◆ Continue to seek social connections
- ◆ Recognize that money is not a primary source of happiness or fulfillment
- ◆ Stay open to reinterpreting your own life experiences
- ◆ Ignore ageism
- ◆ Expand your ideas of beauty, health, age, and sexuality
- ◆ Keep actively engaged in the community
- ◆ Be the change you want to see
- ◆ Embody the admirable characteristics of loved ones who have died

◆ Experience a new (or renewed) relationship with God through Jesus Christ

Reflect on each of the phrases listed above and consider which of them can help you maximize the possibilities that aging offers to you. What will be required of you if you are to really make the most of the possibilities of aging? As people of faith we believe that God created us, invites us to faithful living, and has promised to care for us in this life and the next. The prophet Isaiah reminds us that the Creator God cares for us and will carry us for all of our days: "...listen to me...who have been borne by me from your birth, carried from the womb. . . even when you turn grey I will carry you. I have made, and I will bear; I will carry and will save" (Isaiah 46:3-4). Countless biblical texts suggest that it is God's plan, desire, and provision that each of us live in confidence and peace all of our days. Ultimately, our hope for a life marked with goodness and dignity for every age is met and fulfilled as we place our radical trust in God, who loves us far beyond our ability to comprehend.

Resources

New Beginnings DVD, by Dr. Rick Gentzler (Discipleship Resources, 2005). This 20-minute film presents the individual short stories of older adults and the role their faith plays in their churches and communities.

General Board of Discipleship, Center on Aging & Older Adult Ministries (*www.gbod.org/coa/mission.asp*)

Finding Meaning and Purpose in Life

4

Growing older is filled with both opportunities and challenges. How can we release areas of worry and diminishing capability and embrace new ways to enrich our lives?

Prayer

Almighty God, source of life and author of all meaning and purpose, be for us a strong guide and constant companion as we seek to follow your way and your will. Our desire is to live with an ever-deeper awareness of your presence with us, so that we may live faithfully and joyfully as good stewards of the good gift of life we receive from your hand. So we ask that the mind that was in Christ Jesus may be in us, so that our lives may always be marked with meaning and purpose. Amen.

Scripture

For surely I know the plans I have for you, says the LORD, plans for your welfare and not for harm, to give you a future with hope. Then when you call upon me and come and pray to me, I will hear you.

When you search for me, you will find me; if you seek me with all your heart....

Jeremiah 29:11-13

Martha Hickman, the first contributor to this chapter, is currently moving with her husband from her Tennessee home to a retirement community near her children. Martha began her life challenged with serious childhood illness, grew up, raised a family, lost a child, and became an author and then a delighted grandmother. Now in her senior years and struggling again with physical impairments, Martha shares how she finds joy in the small and great things of daily life.

When I first heard the theme that I was to address in this chapter, it occurred to me that the purpose of growing older was to stay alive! But almost immediately the qualifiers moved in, such as good health, a community of loved ones and friends, enough means to get by, capacity to do some of the things I enjoy, presence of mind to desire and be able to make a positive difference in the lives of others. Well, you get the point, and you can fill in many more of those important qualifiers to experiencing a meaningful life as we grow older.

I have the same anxieties and uncertainties as almost anyone else, maybe more, since I have known in my gut since the age of five, when I was very sick for a long time, that life is fragile and full of surprises, and some of them can be very scary.

However, I do have some thoughts about the issues of aging and have found some approaches to dealing with them in ways that have been helpful to me. I hope that they may be helpful to you.

There it is—growing older—and we need to make our peace with it. This and other chapters will make it clear that we not only need to make our peace with growing older, but also we need to celebrate it, make the most of it, rejoice in it, revel in what it offers, and honestly acknowledge that some losses go along with the many gifts of growing older.

The Many Moods of Aging

Aging is characterized by many moods. The lines from Robert Browning's poem "Rabbi Ben Ezra" come to mind: "Grow old along with me / The best is yet to be." Well, maybe—though my own feeling is that each stage of life is made for itself. Each stage of life has its own meaning and beauty, its own possibilities and opportunities, and its own risks and perils.

There are other moods, too, such as those expressed by the familiar dictum, "Old age is not for sissies," or the declaration of intention, "When I am an old woman I shall wear purple." And then from the Gospel of John: "But when you are old, you will stretch out your hands, and someone will fasten a belt around you and take you where you do not wish to go" (John 21:18).

New Opportunities Come with Age and Wisdom

There are specific tasks and opportunities that come with growing older. There are certain givens, such as retirement, diminishing energy, and often a more limited income, as well as the gradual acquiring of health limitations to our vision, hearing, strength, quickness of thought, and flexibility of our bodies.

But there are also gains and opportunities that come with growing older. We can rearrange our priorities and perhaps for the first time in our lives invest our physical and spiritual energy more fully in the things that really matter to us and that can make this world a better place to live.

We can pay more attention to Being rather than Doing. Every once in a while as I walk down the driveway in the morning

I hear the chatter of the birds and I stop and say, "Good morning, birds." Maybe we can walk a bit more slowly (not only to avoid tipping over—I've done my share of that) just to savor the sounds, sights, and scents of this wonderful world. Now we can find time to observe and experience darkness turn to dawn and then sunrise or to watch the sunset and darkness cover the earth. John Calvin said that nature is "The Theater of God's glory." Now as never before we have time to pay attention and to enjoy this magnificent theater we now call home.

Another important opportunity is the chance to put things in order. So many files, so many stories started, so many letters no longer needed, so many things never used, so many things accumulated but no longer important. Now is the time to place all in priority, decide what you must keep, discard or give to family or Goodwill or your favorite charity what is useful, and recycle the rest. People who have moved to smaller spaces tell me how wonderful it feels to have sorted through and discarded what you no longer need or want. Now is the time to give things away and simplify our lives.

Another opportunity of aging is the option of writing your memoirs. The story of your life is a great gift to your children and grandchildren. Your life is a story that should be told and remembered. My husband is in the process of writing a memoir and takes great delight in reliving chapters of his life. My mother, at my husband's suggestion, wrote down some of the family stories from England, and of her life in America. My father had them typed and gave us ten pages of wonderful stories that we have duplicated and passed on to our children. A friend told me how much he regrets not having his father tell him more about what it was like to emmigrate from Russia and homestead in the United States. As your children and grandchildren grow older, the value of the story of your life will grow exponentially.

Another opportunity that aging affords is more time to spend in silence, meditation, reading, and prayer. A friend does her daily Bible reading and devotion time near an open window. From here, she can contemplate the world around her. One day she reflects on the sights of the garden and street and how they illumine God's word and creation; another day she listens closely to the sounds of the birds, the crickets, and the children's voices, really hearing each note and clamor. You might have time to enjoy the lyrics of a favorite hymn, reading the familiar verses with new meaning and memory.

Now is the time to enjoy the things you have. How many of us have china stored away or lovely gifts still in their boxes? Why not now? Eat your lunchtime sandwich on the good china, wear the Christmas robe, get out those gift towels, and light the beautiful scented gift candle.

Another aim worthy of our attention is to resolve unresolved issues. This past summer my husband and I attended a conference on relationships. A woman in our small group explained she was seventy and she had come to see if she could understand and improve her relationship with her daughter. She painted a bleak picture. She had moved a great distance to be near her daughter and tried every way she knew to establish a loving relationship. But her daughter told her she wished she had not made the move, and furthermore she wished her mother were not her mother. The "coach," as the leader was called, questioned her about the relationship and led her to the suggestion that she phone her daughter, without recrimination or complaint, and tell her she was sorry for anything she might have done to alienate her, and see where the conversation went. The next morning the woman returned. She was practically dancing! She had called her daughter, told her she was sorry for anything she had said or done, but she really wanted to try again. Her daughter replied, "Mother, I want us to be friends, too!" They made arrangements to meet the next week. A cloud of contentment and joy settled over us all. Now is the time to resolve unresolved issues. Not all unresolved areas of our lives will have as happy an ending as those of our friend but knowing that you have made a sincere attempt brings a certain peace and is a way to then release the problem to God.

Grandchildren and Family

On a one-a-day calendar we were given some years ago we found an affirmation that said, "Grandchildren are God's reward for growing older." We didn't have grandchildren at the time, but we were ready. When we learned that our son, John, and his wife were expecting a baby, we were so pleased and excited that we went to a nice restaurant in town to celebrate. Now we have six grandchildren, and of course they are all above average, beautiful, gifted, and healthy. I confess that I am a proud member of the SOGWPIP Society (Silly Old Grandmother With Pictures in Pocket). We know we are blessed.

But we have found that as you add more people to your roster of family the possibility of perils also expands. We worried when our three-month-old grandson spent his first Christmas in the hospital with wheezing and chest congestion. This child is fully recovered, but we know that perils exist and they are not age specific. Who of us expects a child to die? Yet they do. Then grandparents have a double burden. When our daughter was killed in an accident at sixteen, our parents had not only their own pain, but also their pain for us. It is not always an easy ride, being grandparents, but such joy it has brought to our lives.

Letting Go of Worry and Responsibility

It behooves us as we grow older, as it did when we were younger, to cherish the days as they go by, and certainly to forgo worry. Are you the worrier in your house? Several years ago Frederick Buechner had an article in the *Christian Century* on the "Family Worrier," the one who assumes all the worries so other people can be free of them. I am the family worrier. My husband quotes to me, "Worry is the interest we pay on borrowed trouble, most of which never happens." Jesus said, "Do not worry about tomorrow. Today's trouble is enough for today." And while I am learning how to forgo worry, it still creeps in and needs my best effort to cast it out so that I may fully cherish the goodness of each day.

I've had my own struggles with this matter of letting up on vocation. I am a writer, something that I never expected to be when I was growing up, or even in the early years of adulthood. But when the last of our children started school, I began to think of giving it a try. And it has been a very satisfactory second vocation for me. I've written a number of books, including a novel, a collection of short stories, books for young children, a number of personal essay books, including a couple of books on grief. The novel made the biggest splash with large advances in New York and London. But the novel did not do well and disappeared without a trace. Things don't always turn out as we planned or hoped.

I have had aspirations to write another novel. The writer E. L. Doctorow, asked in his mature years whether he thought he would write another novel, said he didn't think he had enough breath. I know what he meant. Energy levels are not what they once were. My husband reminds me that A. A. Milne saw himself as a prominent writer on political issues and was quite disappointed to be remembered as the author of Winnie the Pooh. So my resolve is to set loose to what else may come along, and maybe try to write shorter things, and see what happens.

Mozelle Cor, currently living in a retirement community, is very active in her local congregation's life and ministry and has discovered the gift for painting that has been dormant until now. She shares that her senior years have been the time to try some new things. In a book on aging, Helen Lukes says the ideal is not to do old things less and less well, but to do new things. I think of my widowed sister auditing courses at the university where her husband taught. Learning something new—from literature to plumbing— brings a gift. There are courses in almost every community that can enrich our lives. There are new possibilities even in the morning paper. I want to allow myself the leisure to do the daily crossword puzzle, which is also recommended as a way of keeping our minds sharp. We can take advantage of learning and travel opportunities that are available for older adults. We can learn to do new things, such as discovering a new skill that we didn't know we had. Some have discovered that they were able to do beautiful things with wood, knitting needles, or an artist's paintbrush. This is a time to consider, as Mozelle has, doing some of the things you have always wanted to do but never had time to do. Some of these new things can even be silly. Mozelle shares with us the poem written for a friend on the occasion of her seventieth birthday:

I'd like to add to the mirth and levity
By writing a poem about being seventy
But really I think there's not much to it!
I'll pay more attention whey you reach eighty
I'll write a poem that will be worth the wait-y
That is if I'm around to take note
Now you may think that's too remote
But think how incredibly fast
The sixties decade simply flew past!
Think of all the good things it brought you
Try to recall what the sixties taught you.
As your friend and your elder I have this sage advice

Please watch your step on snow and ice!
And you'll love the seventies!

Other new things can be serious, like keeping a journal, serving in an outreach ministry of your congregation, or keeping an appointment to pray every day for those who have the energy, youth, and skill to carry on ministries of healing, caring, and justice that may require more than we can muster.

An ultimate aspiration of aging is, as a doctor put it to me once, "to make a good exit." Much of the success may come from good medical care, from having kept your life in balance, achieved some of what you dreamt of, and still having people you love and who love you. We may have little control over these factors, but we can try to be in the mood to accept what happens, with the faith and trust that as God has been with us in life, God will be with us through the gateway of death. We can affirm with the Biblical text, "So we do not lose heart. Even though our outer nature is wasting away, our inner nature is being renewed day by day. For this slight momentary affliction is preparing us for an eternal weight of glory beyond all measure, because we look not at what can be seen but what cannot be seen; for what can be seen is temporary, but what cannot be seen is eternal" (2 Corinthians 4:16-18).

Resources

Healing After Loss: Daily Meditations for Working Through Grief, by Martha Hickman (Avon Books, 1999).

Waiting and Loving: Thoughts Occasioned by the Illness and Death of a Parent, by Martha Hickman (Backinprint.com, 2000).

50 Ways to Pray: Practices from Many Traditions and Times, by Teresa Blythe (Abingdon Press, 2006).

5 Getting It All Together Making Decisions

Good planning and open communication with family and friends about medical, financial, and legal decisions are the keys to charting out the life plan we want.

Prayer

God of wisdom, love, and power, we thank you today for the freedom you give us to chart our own course and choose our own way of living. We remember your promise to be our guide and strength in all of life's experiences, so we ask for your help in planning and choosing a way of living that is appropriate for us as your beloved children. We offer our prayers and our lives to you in the name and spirit of Christ. Amen.

Scripture

Do not store up for yourselves treasures on earth, where moth and rust consume and where thieves break in and steal; but store up for yourselves treasures in heaven, where neither moth nor rust consumes and where thieves do not break in and steal. For where your treasure is, there your heart will be also.

Matthew 6:19-21

Mary Boyd is a pilot and a practicing attorney. From her experience helping clients make important life plans, Mary compares planning for the legal, health care, and financial needs of an individual or family to making a flight plan. Mary says, "My husband and I are both licensed and experienced pilots. We enjoy flying and we enjoy flying together. When flying together one of us pilots the plane and the other one operates the radios and navigation equipment. But before we ever begin a flight there are important and essential routine procedures that are *always* followed.

"One of those routine procedures is a thorough checking of the aircraft. This includes everything from oil and fuel supply to flight controls and the surface of the aircraft. The inspection follows a checklist in hand or one securely filed in our memory bank. It is an essential step to make sure the aircraft is ready to fly safely.

"Another one of those essential routines is filing a flight plan. We know where we want to go, but now we must decide the best flight path to follow in order to arrive quickly and safely. Of course, this involves checking the weather and terrain over which we will be flying, places to land en route should that be required, and the weather conditions predicted for our destination. We identify the various radio and visual identification markers along the way that will tell us if we are on course and on time for a safe landing at our destination, or if we have strayed from our desired flight path, will be late, or need to adjust our flight plan."

Planning for living and dying is even more important than planning a flight. Every adult is a candidate for a life plan that will give direction and avoid the dangers of thoughtless or careless actions that could cause harm to the individual and those who love and support that person. While careful planning is needed for every stage of our lives, it becomes even more important as we reach our older adult years. Once again we want to make wise decisions and avoid forcing our children or other family members to make those decisions on our behalf. Regular attention to our plan is essential to make sure things have not changed to the extent that will require an adjustment to our plan.

In this chapter, we'll list legal matters that may need to be considered in order to create a good plan for living. Some of these items are routine and can be easily done; others will require the consultation of family and in other cases professional legal assistance.

Living fully and dying well will not happen without good planning and open communication with all those touched by your life. And even with such planning, the unexpected and unknown can overtake us. Nevertheless, all efforts should be made to live fully and to die well. The purpose of this chapter is to help you do just that.

Wills, Trusts, and Estate Planning

The first thing that often comes to mind is a will. Young and old alike need to have a will that expresses their wishes and is accepted legally in their particular state. One of the first steps will be to name an executor to fulfill the terms of your will. This can be a family member, friend, bank or trust company, or an attorney. It is best to have this person as a resident of the state in which you reside. It is also wise to have a careful inventory of your estate to assure that the executor can carry out your wishes as you direct. This inventory will include personal property, your home, and investments. Letters of instruction may be used for small items such as heirlooms.

Give careful thought about who will be beneficiaries of your estate. Spouse and children are normally listed first but other persons, institutions, or charities may also be included. Be sure to state clearly the amount or items that you wish to go to each beneficiary, including the charities and institutions you have named.

Children need not all be treated equally. Children with special needs may require special provisions. In the case of minor children, when a parent dies all of the estate would normally be left to the surviving spouse. In case of the death of both parents, the will should include a designated guardian for the children. With many families experiencing divorce and remarriage, will-making can be a complex and sensitive issue. Once again it is important to have professional legal help to be certain that your desires can be achieved within the legal parameters set by the state. You may also wish to consult with your spiritual advisor to discern what is fair and equitable for all.

State taxes may vary from state to state. Current federal law exempts one million dollars from estate taxes. Gifts to charity are deductible. If the estate is larger than one million dollars, it is wise to contact an estate-planning attorney for assistance.

Revocable living trusts are being used for special needs cases. They do not save taxes or legal fees but they can assure that bills are paid and property maintained when the person making the will is disabled or a spouse needs special care.

Legal fees and court costs depend on the complexity of the estate and can vary from state to state. Court costs are usually under five hundred dollars unless the will is contested. Legal fees must be approved by the court and are usually less than twelve hundred dollars in small estates and more in large and complex estates. Out-of-family executors may be paid a fee for services. Probate court offices can generally be located in your local government's listing of services.

Holographic wills are wills that are written, signed, and dated by the individual and are not witnessed. These are acceptable in many states if they are entirely in the writing of the person making the will. However, formal wills drawn up by an attorney are safer and offer a greater sense of security for all concerned.

Who's in Charge?

Durable power of attorney allows an individual to name another person to manage financial affairs if the individual becomes disabled. This person may be a family or friend, takes effect on disability, saves the need to set up a conservatorship, and allows another to collect money and pay bills on behalf of the individual granting the Durable Power of Attorney.

Durable power of attorney for health care permits you to name a health care agent who can carry out your wishes should you become unable to do so. State laws vary, so you will need to consult with a legal professional to make certain that your wishes are carried out without confusion.

A living will can give guidance to the person who has your durable power of attorney for health care and will relieve family members of the trauma of cases like that of Terri Schiavo. Your living will should include quality of life issues, treatment issues, organ donation, and other instructions you wish to have carried out should you become unable to make those decisions yourself. A copy of your living will should be shared with your medical providers so your desires are known and can be fulfilled. It should also be shared with family members to eliminate the possibility of confusion and misunderstanding at what may be a stressful time for those who love and care for you.

Again, it is wise to check the laws in your state regarding each of the issues mentioned above and to seek professional help to make certain that your plans will be carried out as you wish and with as little difficulty as possible for those who remain.

Rabbi Earl Grollman, author and speaker on issues of death and dying, describes an ethical will, a personal document that outlines the values, important accomplishments and memories, and the legacy of work that the individual would like to continued by friends and family. This kind of document is a way of telling those who remain how you would like to be remembered and can be a great help to those who plan your memorial service and those who grieve your passing from this life to the next. Of course, your life is the best witness to your values, hopes, and dreams, but putting something on paper for your loved ones can be a great comfort and help. A completed ethical will can be a wonderful document to begin and continue communicating with those you love about your plans to live fully and die well.

Insurance and Health Care Costs

There are other practical decisions that need to be made as we approach and enter our elder years. Perhaps one of the greatest is to plan for our pre-retirement and post-retirement health care. Medicare is the principal health insurance for persons older than sixty-five or who have certain medical disabilities. Currently, ninety-five percent of Medicare beneficiaries are enrolled due to their age. Although Medicare coverage may continue to change, it remains the most used and successful program for elders.

Because of recent changes in Medicare drug benefits and the possibility that other changes will occur, it is wise to check the current situation by calling 1-800-MEDICARE (1-800-633-4227) or your state office on aging and disability.

Choosing Where to Live

Where we choose to live upon retirement may a simple decision for some but can be complicated for others due to health or family requirements. Almost every retiree prefers to maintain an independent lifestyle for as long as possible. How long will you be able to maintain the residence that you now call home? How long will you be able to continue to care for your own needs? When do you think you will need assistance to maintain a good quality of life? These are some of the questions that need to be asked as you make plans for retirement living. Of course, family location and desires are also an important consideration. Living near to children and grandchildren is often a high priority for those considering retirement living plans.

Most of us will have accumulated many more things than we need by the time we reach retirement age. Some of what we accumulate has value only to us other things may have value to family, and still others have some commercial value. While downsizing is never easy, it is often a necessity as we retire and especially as we move to take advantage of the benefits retirement communities provide. Begin downsizing your household belongings sooner rather than later; don't wait until the day you move. When you have the time without the pressure of an upcoming move, you might enjoy beginning to give away some family pieces or special items you no longer need to friends and family. Without the rush, you can enjoy sharing the stories you have about the items and see these belongings happily in use in another home. Imagine seeing the family punch bowl in use at Christmas in a daughter's home or knowing how beautifully a favorite musical instrument is played by a grandchild. Some elders have discovered that this process can best be done over a period of years rather than a period of weeks. As you downsize, be sure to give family members opportunity to tell you what they would like to have as their own.

When fully independent living is no longer feasible or safe, choosing an assisted care living facility or a continuous care facility may be the answer. You may check with your state to find out the level of care a facility is licensed to provide. When checking on costs it is also important to ask about Medicaid and other financial plans that may be available to you.

All of us want to be good stewards of the gift of life, so it is important to include consideration of the contribution you can make to others through offering some of your time to volunteer services. Many communities have special volunteer opportunities including hospital and nursing home visitation, AARP volunteer programs, and mentoring programs for children, youth, and adults. Retirement planning is a good time to visit with your church staff to find out where your particular skills can most effectively be invested.

Wellness and Medical Planning

Dr. David Jarvis is the director of Pulmonary Disease, Critical Care and Sleep Medicine at The Frist Clinic in Nashville, Tennessee. He shares with us that remaining active, good planning and clear communication are the keys to good health and good health care decisions, particularly as we age.

Two key words in this entire discussion are *planning* and *communication*. None of us know when we are going to get sick, be involved in an accident, or die. But we can plan for each of those eventualities in such a way that neither we nor those who care for us will have to make life's most difficult decision when we and others are most unprepared to do so.

To live fully involves care for our physical well being as well as our spiritual well being. If we are fortunate we have been taking care of both for a long time. However, today is always a good time to review our spiritual and physical health and if needed take steps to bring both into a path that leads toward wholeness. We often take health for granted, especially when we are young. The young have an occasional illness, but rarely encounter the health care system except for acute illness that usually quickly resolves. Aging increases our exposure to health care screening and preventive medicine. Finally, health care becomes a big part of our lives as we regularly visit a physician and take numerous medications every day.

We all hope to age a lot, but what is old age anyway? Old age has always been a moving target. In the 1800s, German Chancellor Bismarck mandated sixty-five as the retirement age. It was very likely the first national retirement program. In 1900 the life expectancy was forty-seven, and there were 3.5 million individuals sixty-five years of age or older. In 2004 there were 35 million individuals sixty-five years of age or older, and the life expectancy had increased into the seventies. It is estimated that by 2020 there will be more than one billion people over the age of sixty. Currently the fastest growing segment of the aged includes those over eighty-five years of age. Now only 1 in 5,600 will reach the age of 100. It is estimated that by 2050, 1 in 500 will reach the age of 100.

Life expectancy has changed radically in the last one hundred years. A part of this change has been the result of "better living through chemistry." Vaccines were developed to control many diseases that had proven fatal in the past. More and better drugs became available to treat infection and a variety of diseases and lifestyle and nutrition also contributed to longer life expectancy.

Today the most common medical problems are arthritis, hypertension, heart disease/congestive heart failure, decreased vision and hearing, and diabetes mellitus. The three most common causes of death are heart disease, stroke, and cancer. Cancer is now becoming more prominent as stroke and heart disease decrease because of advances in medical science.

We must remember that dying is a natural part of life, and that in most cases, with good planning and good care, aging and death itself can be done well. In the past, people died in their own homes, surrounded by their families with whom they lived. Today death often occurs in a hospital or nursing home, away from the familiar surroundings once prized and often away from loved ones who were once constant companions. In the past, hospitals were charity institutions for those who did not have a family to care for them. The reason most people die in a hospital or nursing home today simply reflects the truth that in a crisis a hospital is used, and in a chronic illness a nursing home is utilized if the individual can no longer be cared for at home. Deaths from acute illness are diminishing and there is more and more chronic illness with prolongation of life and years.

Individuals usually move to a nursing home when the caregiver no longer has the resources to provide the care required. A spouse may be too frail or a working family member may not be able to afford the time needed to provide the care required. At other times the individual has behavior that is too disruptive or even dangerous for family members to monitor or control. Or perhaps incontinence or some other limitation may make it necessary to enter a care facility.

Having discussions with spouse and children ahead of time can alleviate the stress of making such decisions in the midst of physical upheaval or trauma. It is never too early to consider your own life plan and then to discuss it thoroughly with your spouse and children. Such a discussion will begin the process that you and they will undertake if you are to live fully and die well.

It is never too early and almost never too late to begin planning to live fully and to age gracefully. While it is not always possible to achieve these goals, all efforts should be made to do so. Staying healthy requires effort and work. It is not likely that living fully and aging gracefully will happen by accident or on their own. Staying healthy requires significant effort, as does aging gracefully. The long-standing triad of long life is diet, exercise, and remaining thin. Good genes also help. It is important for each individual to be an active participant in the aging process at every age and stage of life. Physical and mental activity is proven to have a very positive influence on the health and well-being of people of all ages. Exercise prolongs life and improves mental ability while also increasing the quality of life one enjoys. Mental exercises such as social interaction, reading, playing games, and writing are also helpful. It is true that active, involved people live longer, function better, and enjoy life more than those who are inactive and uninvolved. We all need something to focus on and feel good about no matter what our age. Having a mission, goal, or cause about which we care and in which we are involved can add meaning to our lives and improve our well-being. Furthermore, scientific studies show that involvement in religious activities in groups extends life in both quality and years. Good attitudes and effort are important characteristics of those who age gracefully and well.

Older seniors may become isolated and withdrawn, often for reasons beyond their control. Illness, frailty, and physical limitations can be overwhelming and can convince an older senior to stay at home to avoid being embarrassed or injured. When such withdrawl occurs, support by family, friends, and the religious community becomes very important. It is wise for family and other caregivers to establish open communication early in every relationship so that when signs of withdrawal appear, appropriate response can be offered.

Today's seniors are in a much better position to age well than any other generation has been. They are more educated, more financially secure, more vigorous, and more actively involved in their own aging process. Furthermore, they are more socially aware and more involved in more things than ever before. Today's seniors also have more freedom and more choices in directing their own health care and life decisions.

Summing It Up

Most of us have been working at "getting it all together" for a long time, and we know by heart many of the items we have discussed in this chapter. In that case we may need just a little tweaking of our way of life to bring us to that maximum quality of life that we seek at every age. If after a review of our own situation we discover there is more to be done to get it all together, now is the perfect time to get started by making a list of the things you want to do to enhance communication and continue your planning to live fully and die well.

Resources

Setting My House in Order: A Record of my Current Medical Needs, by Bernice Monter (Abingdon Press, 2004).

Ethical Wills: Putting your Values on Paper, by Dr. Barry Baines (Perseus Publishing, 2001).

Our Greatest Gift, by Henri J. M. Nouwen (HarperSanFrancisco, 1994).

No Finer Way to Die, by Kathleen Adcock Haskett (Choices in Print Publishing, 2005).

6 Dying Well

Dying well means something different for each person. For many of us, it means being at peace with our lives, with the past, with our family and friends, and with our dreams. Planning and preparation help to ensure that we will feel a sense of order and readiness so when we die we can be where we'd like to be and with the people we love.

Scripture

Do not let your hearts be troubled. Believe in God, believe also in me. In my Father's house there are many dwelling places. If it were not so, would I have told you that I go to prepare a place for you? And if I go and prepare a place for you, I will come again and will take you to myself, so that where I am, there you may be also. John 14:1-4

Prayer

Life giving God, thank you for offering life abundant and eternal to all who seek your face. We accept your offer and ask for your guidance, strength, and help to assist us to live faithfully and fully every day of our lives. And we ask that you will guide us and strengthen us as we make the transition from this life to the next. Hold us close to yourself, do not let us ever stray from your side, and grant us the joy of abundant and eternal life every day in this beautiful world and in the dwelling that even now you are preparing for us.
    Amen.

No living person escapes the universal experiences of birth and death. Both are natural parts of life that should be respected, prepared for, studied, understood, and celebrated. Neither can be denied or ignored without serious and needless negative consequences. Preparation and understanding can limit the stress, anxiety, and fear that often accompany birth and death.

We often make extravagant preparation for birth but seldom make the same kind of preparation for death. Hospitals and clinics that specialize in obstetrics have numerous classes to prepare parents and family members for the great mystery of birth. These classes cover everything from exercise, diet, and bodily changes during pregnancy to the emotional stress of bringing a child into the world.

Preparation for death is not so well or so widely done. There are some legitimate reasons for this. Sometimes death comes unannounced; there is no nine-month gestation period with ample signs that it is time to get ready. Even when we are old and full of years, it is hard to determine when the final day or final breath will come. Sometimes our preparation is put off because death seems to be a contradiction of the deep hunger for life in the human heart. However, since we all know that we will all die, why not prepare for death as we prepare for birth?

My two brothers were born in our family's two-room house. I was born in my uncle's house with a physician present, a first in our family. Most of the preparation for these births happened within the family. My grandparents all died at home, and the immediate family provided preparation for death and care during the dying process. I imagine there was little denial about the reality of death in that culture. But by the time my parents died, both in a hospital, the process of denying the reality of death was well under way, and I believe it has rapidly accelerated since then.

When my father died, his doctor—who knew me—called and said, "Your father expired," and then gave me the details of his death. When my mother died, a nurse called at two in the morning and used the same phrase. I know their words were offered with the best of intentions, but death is not like a magazine subscription that we can overcome with a check to the publisher. Death is our final—and some would even say our most triumphant—act of life in this world. But it will not be repeated or followed with another eighty years of life, as we know it today.

The most significant reason for our silence is most likely the blanket of denial that our culture uses to hide the reality of death and even of aging. Enormous efforts are made to preserve our youth and then to appear younger than we really are. Everything from makeup to various kinds of cosmetic surgery is promoted to keep us looking young, and the industry that provides funeral services makes heroic efforts to deny the reality of death. We try to find gentler words than "he died," so we say "he passed" or "he went home to be with God." All appropriate, but also probably a way of masking or denying the reality of death.

The church has been amazingly silent in this process. We who hold the good news that life is eternal have been slow to share that good news with each other, much less the rest of the world. How can it be that we, who follow the One who promised to prepare a place for us and who welcomed the thief on the cross beside him into paradise, say so little about the eternal nature of life and of our mortality in this life?

One of the most formidable reasons is that only one person has returned to tell us the promise is true. If we are uncertain about that One, we may be reluctant to proclaim his message. Some fear that if we give attention to the eternal nature of life, we will appear otherworldly and may neglect to live in such a way that God's reign will be realized in this life as well as in the next.

But the reality of death and the promise of the gospel compel us to go further and prepare for a good death as carefully and as wisely as we prepare for a good birth. Previous chapters have covered many of the important facets of preparation for living fully and dying well. In this chapter we will consider what a good death is like and how we can prepare for it.

What do you want to happen and to experience as you approach and begin your final act of living? Who would you like to be with you during this last great mystery? What are the things that you want to make sure have been taken care of in preparation for your death? How would you like your life to be celebrated after your death? What do you fear and what do you anticipate? What are the emotional, physical, mental, and spiritual aspects of dying that you wonder about? What other questions do you have about dying well?

Some Choices We Can Make

After a more than three-year struggle with brain cancer, my brother's primary care physician told him that the disease had outpaced all treatment options, including radiation and chemotherapy. The illness was terminal. My brother, never being slow to respond, replied, "I know I am terminal. So are you. We all are dying. But how long do I have to live?" This was a wonderful and critical moment in preparation for dying. If the doctor had denied the reality of the situation, it would have been much more difficult for my brother to complete his very personal and very important preparation for the final act of his life in this world.

The doctor said he did not know, but he would study all the scans and test results and meet with him the following week to talk about it. In this appointment—his last with a doctor—my brother again asked for a time frame. The doctor responded, "It could be days or weeks or months, but most likely weeks." It was then that the conversation turned to hospice care, and several hours later the arrangements had been made to fulfill my brother's request to take his last breath in his own home. Ten weeks later his desire was realized as he died in a familiar environment, surrounded by family, friends, and his favorite hospice nurse.

My brother's death could be described as good. He had lived a long and full life. He was at peace with God, the world, his life, and his approaching death. He had struggled with cancer for three years, and he was very tired and wanted to die. He was not only full of years but also full of faith and anticipated his final homecoming.

But all death does not come at the end of a long illness or because of old age. The death of a child is an unfathomable loss that is under every circumstance difficult and painful beyond description. A deep and abiding faith gives hope and comfort in the midst of the pain, but it does not deny the reality of death. Death is not to be taken lightly at any age—even Jesus wept at the death of his friend Lazarus—but as the Scripture says, we are not as those without hope. For Christians, death is the end of life in this world, but it is never the end of life. Therefore, as Christians we commend our loved ones, young and old, to the loving care of our faithful Savior who promised even the thief beside him on the cross an immediate place in paradise.

When death approaches slowly and surely, we have more reason and time to focus on preparation and readiness. When it comes suddenly and unannounced, preparation time is limited or nonexistent. Therefore, it is especially important for the church to invite everyone into the full discussion of life that includes birth and death. With very young children this teaching may best be done in the circle of family. But by the time children reach elementary school, they are good candidates for learning more formally about the beginning and ending of living in this world. Of course, this teaching must be done wisely, gently, and with age-appropriate language and images. But this kind of education can equip them for a lifetime of confident living, aware of their mortality, but not intimidated by this last great mystery of living in this world.

What Does It Mean to Die Well?

Dying well will mean being at peace with our life and our death, our companions on this earthly journey, and our God who has given us life, sustained us in all our days, and promises to be with us always.

Dying well will mean having all of our business matters cared for and in order with clear instructions for those who remain and will carry out our wishes.

Dying well will mean careful management of pain, balancing our desire to be relatively pain-free with our desire to preserve our clarity of mind to experience our last days with as much comfort, joy, and participation in living as possible.

Dying well will mean a calmness and tranquility that comes with careful preparation for our transition from one home to the next. This calmness and tranquility is not only available to the person experiencing dying but to those who lovingly watch as a dear one slips beyond the horizons of the world we know so well.

Dying well will mean having those we choose—likely family, friends, and those who have helped us in our spiritual journey—to experience this final act with us.

The hospice movement has been a leader in preparing persons for the experience of death. Through research, study, careful observation, and many years of experience, they have learned how to evaluate the process of dying and some of the work that seems to be universally done as we prepare to die. They have learned from the works of people such as Dr. Elizabeth Kuebler-Ross, who outlined the five stages a person experiences when knowingly approaching death (denial, bargaining, anger, depression, and acceptance). Some of the resources hospice care and others offer are listed in the bibliography at the end of this chapter.

In death as in life we are unique. And no person's experience is exactly like another's. We all have images of what this great mystery will be like, but the truth is no one but God knows fully what this experience is like. Stories can sometimes carry the weight of truth too great for words. The following story may bring to your mind and heart important truth as you consider your own mortality and the promise of the gospel.

When our first grandson was about three years old, he and his mother came to our home in the woods for the evening meal. They arrived early and his father was working late, so his mother and grandmother suggested that I take Sam for a walk in the woods.

It was autumn, and we stuffed the pockets of the jackets we were wearing to keep us warm full of black walnuts before we made our way into the woods. The sun had set as we made our way down a steep incline to a small pond. There we stopped and Sam squealed with delight as he threw nut after nut into the pond and laughed with pleasure after each splash.

Soon we were out of nuts, and Sam took my hand as we began our climb up the hill toward home. It was nearly dark, and the woods were scary to a three-year-old. Sam grabbed my leg and said, "Grandpa, hold you." It was his way of saying, "Carry me."

I picked him up and rested his weight on my left hip. With my left arm low across his body and my right arm across his shoulders, we continued our slow climb up the hill.

Occasionally Sam would turn around and look up the hill, but there was nothing but deep darkness and unknown mystery.

However, after a few more minutes of walking he looked around again and saw lights through the leaves.

And quick as a flash of light he shouted out, "Grandmas house!" He wriggled to get down and walk beside me once more.

He reached up and we walked hand in hand out of the darkness of the woods, across the lawn, up the back steps, and into the warmth, light, and love of home.

It is a journey we will all make, and there is nothing to fear as we walk hand in hand with the One to whom we belong, our faithful Savior in this life, in death, and in life that never ends.

Who could ask for more?

Thanks be to God, it is enough!

Resources

Final Gifts: Understanding the Special Awareness, Needs, and Communications of the Dying, by Maggie Callanan and Patricia Kelley (Bantum Dell, 1997).

On Death and Dying: What the Dying Have to Teach Doctors, Nurses, Clergy, and Their Own Families, by Elisabeth Kubler-Ross (Touchstone Press, 1969).

7 *What Happens When We Die?*

As Christians, we believe in eternal life, but don't often talk of that last act of life in this world. While each person's death is as unique as their birth, what can we learn from others' experiences about the transition from life to everlasting life?

Scripture

Now faith is the assurance of things hoped for, the conviction of things not seen. Indeed, by faith our ancestors received approval. By faith we understand that the worlds were prepared by the word of God, so that what is seen was made from things that are not visible.... They confessed that they were strangers and foreigners on the earth, for people who speak in this way make it clear that they are seeking a homeland.... But as it is, they desire a better country, that is, a heavenly one. Therefore God is not ashamed to be called their God; indeed, he has prepared a city for them.

(Hebrews 11:1-3, 13b-14, 16)

Prayer

Eternal God, we thank you for your grand design of life abundant and eternal.

We pray for grace and faith to trust you enough to live the abundant life fully in this world and one day to follow you unafraid into our true and eternal home. We offer our prayers and our lives to you in the name and spirit of Christ. Amen.

As Christians, we proclaim and celebrate our core belief and our fundamental hope that life is eternal. Life does not end when our body stops functioning. Life goes on—at a different level, to be sure, but it does go on. We must remind each other often that birth and death are normal and natural consequences of living; everyone experiences both.

Huston Smith was asked if at eighty-six years of age he was afraid to die. He replied, "No, I'm pretty much ready for it. I do not want to be dependent upon others and I am fearful of pain, but I have no fear of death. I believe with all great religions that death is as natural as a leaf falling from a tree in autumn."

Huston Smith is a devout Christian, a United Methodist and world religion scholar known and respected around the world. He reflects the view of all major world religions that death is a natural and not-to-be-feared consequence of life. Christians proclaim that life is eternal and continues from what is now familiar to that which at the moment is unknown.

Christianity at its core teaches that we are spiritual beings as well as physical beings and that we live and die in the presence of the One who is forever beyond us and forever with us. Therefore, Christians face death with peace and assurance at the very depth of their being. You and I belong to God, and no event, disease, disaster, or even death itself can take us out of the loving embrace of our Creator.

Even in a world torn asunder by greed, violence, and shrill voices, Christians are filled with hope and confidence that all is well and all will be well because we live in God's world and we are God's children. As Paul before us, we too can say that we live, move, and have our being in God, who is ever beyond us and always within us and always with us (Acts 17:28).

We declare that death is not a poor outcome of life but a natural part of life that provides transition from this world as we know it to the world prepared for us from the beginning of time. As the Scriptures remind us, we leave a city built with human hands and arrive at a city not made with hands (Hebrews 11:16).

Christians recognize the reality of death and the pain of sorrow and grief. And we remember that Jesus, knowing what he did of God, death, and life eternal, still wept at the death of his dear friend Lazarus. Up to the very last, Jesus asked that the cup of his own crucifixion be taken away. We also remember the words of Jesus proclaiming that we are "children of the resurrection," and therefore we recognize the reality of eternal life as well (Luke 20:36).

When Nels Ferre was teaching at Andover Newton Seminary, one of his students called him at midnight because their little baby had just died. Dr. Ferre went to the small student apartment and sat with the grieving parents for two hours. Not many words were spoken, but when this wise professor stood to leave he said, "God is crying, too" (*Perspectives*, January 2006, Holland, MI).

The Bible says we have a loving, caring God who knows us, understands us, and always embraces us with divine love. The writer of Hebrews strains to make this clear: "...we do not have a high priest who is unable to sympathize with our weaknesses, but we have one who in every respect has been tested as we are, yet without sin" (Hebrews 4:15). Dying is our final homecoming to be with the One who fully understands us and loves us still. Of course, there is regret to leave those we love, and we do experience sorrow as we say goodbye for a time to those companions and loved ones who have been so important in our lives. In *The Dance of Life: Weaving Sorrows and Blessings Into One Joyful Step*, Henri Nouwen put it this way: "But when the time has come for our dying and death, let us rejoice that we can go home and be united with the One who calls us the beloved" (Ave Maria Press, 2006; page 183).

In the chapter "Dying Well," we thought about the difference between the death of a child, the death of a person at the peak of their powers, and the death of one as I am, full of years and with a lifetime of good memories and good experiences. We reflected on what a good death would require. In this chapter we want to think together about what happens when we die.

For some who read these paragraphs, death has been a recent visitor, as loved ones and dear ones slipped the bonds of both the joy and the pain of earth for a world unknown to our eyes but rich in the promise of God. And for some, such as pastors and medical professionals, death has been a frequent visitor, as vocation brought us into the experience of death with those in our care.

Although all of us think of our own death and the deaths of those we love, we spend little time talking openly, honestly, gently, and wisely about this most mysterious and final act of living in this world. For the most part we are left unprepared for what our faith proclaims as our most glorious moment, that moment when we experience life at its very fullest, life no longer fragmented and incomplete but whole and complete. Eternal life, now begun, will then be fully realized.

The Mystery of Death

As people of faith we speak very little about what actually happens when we die. Death is such a great mystery, and for some such a great fear, that we find it awkward to begin talking about death to anyone but our most trusted companions, and sometimes not even to them. We must be honest in such a conversation and recognize that there is so much that we do not know about the process of dying or about death itself. Medical professionals may have a better grasp on the physical markers that tell us when our bodies begin to shut down, and the social sciences may be able to tell us some of the psychological work that is going on, and wise spiritual guides may be able to help us see both the resources and the pathway of the spirit in this movement from this world to the next. But seldom have these gifts been brought together in the church for honest reflection, gentle and loving conversation, and new discovery. This discussion is what we are about during these weeks of thinking about living fully and dying well.

We have an enormous amount of anecdotal evidence that is the experience of many who have observed death close up and those who have had near death experiences and have returned to tell about it. There have been numerous studies of these experiences, but for the most part they are not discussed because death is not discussed. I am sure that many who are reading these paragraphs have had mystical experiences, and I am sure there are some who have had near death experiences. But seldom do we have the opportunity or the environment in which we can share at the trusting level necessary to talk about life and death issues.

Often we are fearful of talking about our own mystical experiences because we think we will be dismissed as a little "too spiritual" or a little "too crazy" to be trusted. We have some fear of being seen as too mystical in an intellectual culture or too mystical in a scientific world. But as Huston Smith says in *The Soul of Christianity*, we are physical beings, but we are also spirit. Science relies on our physical senses, mostly our vision, for its discoveries. But there are some things that our physical senses do not detect. Nobody has ever seen a thought. Nobody has ever seen a feeling. And yet, the world of our thoughts and feelings is the primary world in which we live. (HarperSanFrancisco, 2005). Silence about our own mystical experiences, the things we cannot see, or our own death, is not a good way to deal with our deepest experiences or our deepest questions. So we will examine some of that large body of experience that has been collected and preserved, reflect upon it, learn from it, and engage others in conversation about this most important part of our lives. Sharing your own experience with others may be the most helpful thing that can happen as we lose our fear of speaking about death or other experiences that are at the very core of our being but almost too sacred to talk about.

Jesus said, "Do not let your hearts be troubled. Believe in God, believe also in me. In my Father's house there are many dwelling places. If it were not so, would I have told you that I go to prepare a place for you?" (John 14:1-2). There can be no doubt about the certainty that these words of Jesus proclaim about life after death.

David Shofer, facing his own death from cancer, said his mother told him that everyone wants to get to heaven but no one wants to die to get there. But for the informed Christian, the transition from this life to next is not to be feared but to be faced. Faced openly, honestly, with hope and deep and abiding faith in the One who gives life. To do so requires that we look at what we do know about the process and experience of dying. We will look briefly at near-death experiences, the work of preparing to die, and the signs that death is near. The bibliography includes some of the resources available for those facing death and those watching and waiting with the dying.

Near-Death Experiences

I have been privileged to be with a number of people as they prepared for death and with some when they experienced death. For some death occurred—that is their heart stopped beating—but they were revived and lived to tell about it. In almost every instance the experience is described as deeply moving and affirming. Near-death experiences have been carefully studied, and in 1998 the estimate was that there were thirteen million adults in the United States who had a near-death experience with at least some of the typical markers (*What Happens When I Die: A Study of Life and Death,* by George Hoover; Abingdon Press, 2004; page 15). In 2001, *The Lancet* published the findings of a ten-year research project led by

Dutch cardiologist Pim can Lommel, who discovered that 18 percent of 344 patients who had been declared clinically dead reported a near-death experience after being revived. These patients were interviewed two years later and again eight years later. All remained unafraid of death and reported to have a higher degree of emotional vulnerability and intuitive ability. (ODE, December 2005). Some will say that this is a purely physiological reaction to chemical changes in the brain. Others would argue that it is the world of evil and darkness and we should not even discuss the subject. Most of us fall somewhere between these two extremes. When we visit with someone who has had such an experience, we usually find a person who is very much in love with life and very much *not* afraid to die.

There are as many different experiences of near death as there are of life itself. Each one of us is unique and our experience of life is unique, so why wouldn't our experience of transition from this life to the next also be unique?

There are some general experiences that many people in these situations share. No one person has them all, but some have many. These experiences that often precede death include the following:

The experience of entering a beautiful light.

The experience of seeing loved ones or acquaintances who have died.

The experience of seeing Jesus or God.

The experience of a wonderful peace and tranquility.

The experience of reluctance to return to life on earth.

The experience of seeing heaven.

The experience of wonderful happiness and contentment.

The experience of a great desire to do good in the world.

Occasionally people describe frightening experiences where they seem trapped by their own anger or desires. Others tell of conversion, of experiencing forgiveness and transformation and being filled with compassion for the world and all people.

Most will say that they no longer believe in life after death; now they *know* there is life after death. And they live their lives more fully and see death as a friend and not the last great enemy.

Beverly and I had the privilege of being near our sister-in-law when she died of brain cancer. She was a devout Christian and had no fear of death. As she grew weaker in hospice care, she began to report to her husband that she had visitors in her room. She spoke of the beautiful flowers, the wonderful views that she was able to see. When she said that their neighbor who had recently died came to visit, my brother asked, "Well, what did he have to say? What did he tell you?" And so typical for her, she said, "You know me, I did most of the talking!" A few days later she died with her children holding her hands. Her husband was in the hospital at the time and died a short time later.

My mother, a daughter of immigrants who married an immigrant from Russia, was in failing health for many years and lived with our family for twelve years before she went to a nursing home for fifteen months before her death. She was taken from the nursing home in a coma to the local hospital. My wife went to see her, as I was out of town. The doctors advised against calling my brothers to come to see her; they lived fifteen hundred miles away and she would likely not wake up before she died. While she was in a coma, she murmured the German words, *"Ich muss heim gehen"* and then *"ess ist zo shoen"*. With my limited German language skills I translated this to mean, "I must go home. It is so beautiful."

When I returned home, I saw her in this deep coma and assumed the prognosis that she would never awaken was correct. But much to everyone's surprise she woke up. My mother, who had never been easy to live with, now seemed to be a different person. Each of her children and grandchildren who knew her would say she was a wonderful cook, but none would say she was easy to get along with. The most remarkable thing was that when she awakened from the coma, she was sweet, gentle, humorous, and delightful.

She was incredibly weak, but when I asked if she knew she had been speaking in German, she replied that she knew. And when I asked her if she knew what she said while in a coma, she replied, "Yes." So I asked, "Were you talking about your childhood home when you said you had to go home?" And she replied, "No, I was talking about my heavenly home." "Well," I said, "were you there?" "No," she said, "but I could see it and it is so beautiful." She was a transformed person who was at peace with herself, her world, her family, and I believe with God.

The next morning at two A.M. her heart stopped. I believe she is as much alive today as you are as you read these paragraphs.

Doing The Work Of Preparing To Die

There are many studies about the interior work that we do as we prepare to die. The hospice movement has been very helpful in not only observing this work but also in sharing some of their findings with the rest of us. I am personally indebted to hospice staff and hospice printed resources for my own understanding and learning about dying and death. To observe hospice staff working with those I love was at every point a positive experience.

To some degree we have already talked about doing the work of preparing to die in the previous chapters. But in most instances that work was the *external* work that we do to prepare to die. That external work is absolutely essential to living fully and to dying well. It is work that should be done. But there is *internal* work that also goes on, and it too is essential for a good death. It is a good thing to know what I am experiencing as I die, and it is good for those who watch my approaching death with me to know what is going on in my interior life as well as my physical life.

Let me quote from *The Final Act of Living* by Barbara Karnes. She is a long time hospice nurse and this text is frequently used by hospice workers.

"There are a lot of similarities between birth and death…We go through labor to get into this world and we go through labor to leave it. The labor to leave this world is harder on us, the watchers, than on the person who is doing the labor. The person who is dying is so removed from their body that they do not experience physical sensations in a normal way…. Some women in labor sneeze and out pops the baby; other women, thirty-six hours later are still trying to push the little guy out. So it is with the labor to leave this world. Some of us can get out our bodies more easily than others." (Barbara Karnes Books, Inc., 2003; page 256–57)

◆

My last living brother died last September. I was with him in July and helped him make arrangements for hospice home care, and then in September Beverly and I were with him until just a short time before he died. At different times as we sat with him he reported seeing his wife and my brother, although I could see no one. I saw only my brother in his hospital bed in his own living room, but he saw all three of us there together. He lived many of his last days in these two worlds of reality. Who is to say what he saw was less real than what I saw? While I was unable to see what he saw, for him the reality of these visitors was unquestioned.

My brother also revisited his business that he had sold twenty years ago and seemed to rehearse previous business decisions, giving instructions on how things should be done. He was a WWII veteran who was wounded on Okinawa and relived those experiences that for the first ten years after the war regularly awakened him with nightmares.

I had taken him to a number of offices around town to make sure all was in order to sell his house. The executor of his estate came to his home to review his wishes and to make sure that she understood fully what was to be done. Late one evening he asked me to call her and then took the phone and gave her last minute instructions on what he wanted done for his daughter, granddaughter, and great-grandson in the interim between his death and the distribution of his estate. He was doing that exterior and interior work of preparing to die. For days he appeared to sleep in his recliner and was disengaged from conversation around him. If we spoke his name he would respond but within seconds was once again disengaged, doing that interior work of preparing to die. Hospice workers suggested that to some degree he was already living in that other world for which he longed.

Our own experience of dying will be as unique as we are. We don't look alike, walk alike, or think alike, and we don't die alike. But we do share many of these significant experiences, and one of them is the interior work of preparing to die. Some do it quickly, others slowly. Some who die suddenly may need to do it while already living in the next world. We do not know. We only know we trust the One who told us that a dwelling place is being prepared for us by the One who loves us. Whether our death is sudden and unexpected or slow with time for all the interior and exterior work to be done, the end result is the same. We live and die in the embrace of God's love that can never fail or forsake.

Signs of Approaching Death

Signs of approaching death are obvious to the health care professional and certainly to the professional hospice workers. One of the signs that those near to us will notice is that as we approach death we tend to withdraw from the world around us.

Even close family members may sense that we are disconnecting from this world and no longer want visitors that at one time would have been eagerly entertained.

This withdrawal may include a desire to have the television off or the once loved music turned down. My brother, who had his television on for sixteen hours a day, gradually disengaged from the news and weather that he always wanted to see. During his final days he did not want the television on at all. One of the early days of his withdrawal process, he had nine friends who came to see him. He then named just a few who should be invited in to see him on a regular basis.

Barbara Karnes, in *The Final Act of Living*, reminds us that along with withdrawal from the world there is also withdrawal from food and even water. As the body begins to shut down the need and desire for food just goes away. We do need to eat to live but as we prepare to die we lose the desire or the need to eat. To try and force food is generally not successful or helpful. At this point our need is for spiritual food and spiritual energy. The quiet reading of favorite scripture passages, the singing of a favorite hymn, the sound of much loved music, the spoken and silent prayers of trusted friends, and the loving words and gentle touch of loved ones can offer nourishment to the soul and spirit of the one experiencing death. These acts can also be a source of healing and mending for the brokenness and sorrow of those of us who remain.

Disorientation is another sign of approaching death. Some remain lucid and clear-thinking until the last breath. Others show signs of disorientation and confusion about where they are and what is going on. Often medication for pain can trigger or exaggerate the disorientation that is a part of this final act of dying.

There are changes in the body as death approaches, changes that begin to be visible even to the untrained eye. Blood pressure falls and pulse, temperature, breathing, and skin color change. Breathing is often complicated by congestion that results in unusual sounds in the chest and throat. Restlessness with frequent movement of the arms and hands is not uncommon. And finally when the heart stops and there is an order not to resuscitate, the work of dying is complete. We have left this city made with hands for a new and beautiful home not made with hands. That is the core of our belief as Christians.

The subject of what happens when we die is not easily or often talked about in our culture, but it should be and must be talked about if we are to live fully, claiming our inheritance as children of a God of love. At the very center of our faith is the God of love, who leads us and will not let us go in this life and will not forsake us as we pass through the valley of the shadow of death to the city of light and life prepared for all who love God.

Homecoming

My life on our family farm was good. We were incredibly poor, but so was everyone else. I wore my brother's shoes, shirts, and pants, as did everyone else who had an older brother. We had no near neighbors and seldom saw other children so school was a wonderful experience, although it was two and a half miles away if we followed the best road and much shorter if we walked across the fields.

We usually rode a horse to school, as did the other children who attended with us. The barn on the school ground was filled with hay every fall and our horses were inside eating while we were in school. In the spring, when my father and older brother needed the horses in the field, my next oldest brother and I walked to and from school.

School was dismissed at four in the afternoon and I would walk the short way home, unless there was too much water from melting snow; then I would follow the road. But either way I would approach our farmstead from a small hill. When I got to the top, there was our house about three blocks away.

I would begin running down that hill, unbuttoning my jacket, and if it was warm, my shirt. I burst into the kitchen that was filled with the aroma of fresh bread or cookies prepared by my mother, just waiting for my arrival.

I loved school, the excitement of learning and the fun of being with other children, but there was no place like home and the loving welcome for me there. So I slipped off my clothes as I ran the last few blocks, ready to take off my "school clothes" and put on my "home clothes."

One day you will hear that Rueben has died. Let there be no sorrow, but instead celebration as you remind each other, "He just slipped out of his school clothes and put on his home clothes. He is at home now."

Thanks be to God for the good news we share in Christ.

Resources

The Dance of Life: Weaving Sorrows and Blessings Into One Joyful Step, by Henri Nouwen (Ave Maria Press, 2006).

The Soul of Christianity, by Huston Smith, (HarperSanFrancisco, 2005).

The Final Act of Living—Reflections of a Long Time Hospice Nurse, by Barbara Karnes (BKBooks.com, 2003).

What Happens When I Die: A Study of Life and Death, by George Hoover (Abingdon Press, 2004).

Mrs. Hunter's Happy Death, by John Fanestil (Doubleday, 2006).

From the author: "I am indebted to Barbara Karnes and her book, *The Final Act of Living:Reflections of a Longtime Hospice Nurse*, and to George Hoover and his book, *What Happens When I Die?* for much of the insight for this chapter and for helping me in my journey toward a greater understanding of the mystery of dying."

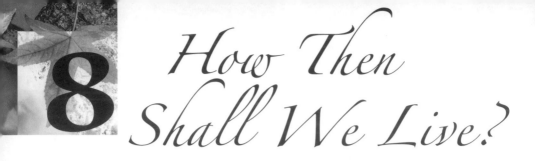

8 How Then Shall We Live?

How will you recreate your life to live fully, joyfully, and productively as long as life in this world lasts? Living fully now helps us approach our final journey into the eternal life to come with assurance, faith, and peace, with trust in the God who loves us always.

Scripture

As God's chosen ones, holy and beloved, clothe yourselves with compassion, kindness, humility, meekness, and patience. Bear with one another and, if anyone has a complaint against another, forgive each other; just as the Lord has forgiven you, so you also must forgive. Above all, clothe yourselves with love, which binds everything together in perfect harmony.

Colossians 3: 12-14

Prayer

Everlasting God and Companion of all people, past and present, we give you thanks for your transforming work within generations past and now within us who seek your face today. Grant to us grace and strength to live fully and faithfully as your children in this world. And when our life in this world ends, may the light of your presence guide us through the valley of the shadow of death and into the light, love, and joy of our eternal home. We offer our prayer and our lives in the name and spirit of Christ. Amen.

In previous chapters we have faced our own mortality and have thought about the two universal experiences of all humans, birth and death. We have considered the mystery and wonder that can be found in both. We celebrate every new birth with joyful recognition and we welcome each new life in our midst with confidence and hope. It is thoroughly appropriate to celebrate death with the same joyful recognition of new life welcomed into our eternal home prepared for us by the One who alone has power to give life. Death, as birth, is filled with hope for those whose lives are given to God in faith and trust.

For Christians, the sting of death has been removed and replaced with the peace of living at home with God in this world and the next. All through our lives as Christians, we learn how to relinquish and more fully abandon our lives to God. It is wonderful if we can begin this process early, while we are still young and have years and years to practice what we have come to believe. If we are granted long life, our life with God is even more rich, fulfilling and life giving. As we enjoy the freedom from vocational demands, we may find the time and energy to focus more clearly on life and its meaning and find new ways to invest our lives for good in the world.

Living fully is life's most rewarding gift. Young or old, rich or poor, at the peak of our powers or weakened by the limitations of age or disease, living fully is something that in our better moments we all desire and with God's help can all achieve. With careful and determined preparation, it is a gift we can all receive and enjoy. Just as we cannot live fully without serious consideration of life and its meaning, we cannot die well without consideration of death and its meaning for us all.

In this final chapter we will consider how we—young, old, or middle aged—can fashion our lives in such a way that we may live fully, joyfully, and fruitfully as long as life in this world lasts. We want to be living in such a way that we can approach our final act on earth and enter the world to come filled with assurance, confidence, hope, peace, and abiding faith and trust in the God who loves us always. Ephesians declares that we have "received an inheritance in Christ" (Ephesians 1:11). It is an inheritance that is given by God and cannot be taken from us. An inheritance that assures us of a loving and abiding relationship with the One who alone is the author of life, abundant and eternal. To live "in Christ" as the Bible invites us to do is to be able to die "in Christ" as well. Such living and such dying are marked by an ever-greater abandonment of life to God and an ever-greater confidence and trust in God for all things.

Our Spiritual Journey

We seldom discover by accident how to live, just as we do not discover by accident how to die well. We are all spiritual beings whose spiritual life is more like a journey than a destination. We do not arrive and then have nothing more to learn or do. Rather, once we recognize and give our consent to God's presence in our lives, we begin a relationship that never ends. It is a relationship that continues to grow in meaning and significance as long as life lasts. This growing relationship naturally leads to ever-greater trust, confidence, love, hope, peace, and companionship with God. It is a relationship begun in this world that continues in the world to come.

A pastor friend of mine observed that the people under his care died just about the way they lived. It is not a surprising discovery. Persons who are at peace with God and seek to live in harmony with God will likely die at peace with God and in harmony with God. They are the persons who have realized that they have never lived outside of God's loving presence, even though they may have often forgotten that they were in God's presence. These are the persons who through the years have fashioned a trusting and obedient relationship with God.

They have sought to be faithful to God's direction and have claimed for themselves the rich promises of God, never to forsake them in this life or the life to come.

Now that we know who we are—spiritual beings and objects of our Creator's incomprehensible love—we can look honestly at the rest of our identity. We are also mortal creatures whose life in this present form is limited. We are free persons who can live and grow in relationship with God for all time, and we have the capacity to respond daily to God's love and grace. We also know that we can turn aside, distracted by many voices that sometimes hush the voice of God calling for our attention and love.

When I was a small boy on our North Dakota farm, before we had a tractor my father did all of the planting and harvesting with horses. In the springtime he would plow with five horses hitched to a two-bottom plow from early morning until near dark. When I returned home from school, I would quickly change my clothes, do my chores, and run to where my father was plowing in the field. I followed him, walking in the furrow behind the plow, until dark when he would stop, bring in the horses, and feed them before we went to our small two-room house where we shared the evening meal as a family.

I enjoyed the time of planting most of all, because the drill that was used to plant the seed was pulled by four horses and had a platform on each side of the implement on which the driver could stand and make certain that the horses followed the mark of the wheel made the time before. This was to assure that nothing would be left unseeded and nothing would be seeded twice. I liked seeding time the best because I could stand on one of those platforms while my father stood on the other. Some times the cold North Dakota wind whipped the dirt off the wheel that was close to the platform on which I stood. With my face stung by the dirt and my body shivering with cold, my father would try to persuade me to go home and get warm. But despite the discomfort, despite the cold, I stood there near my father, until he unhitched the horses and we went home together. Why did I endure the cold, discomfort, and my own weariness? The answer is simple, I wanted to be near to the one who loved me and cared for me in every circumstance.

Living in Companionship with God

Once we discover who we are as children of God, once we experience the companionship of God in Christ and know the fulfillment of living in faithful and growing relationship with God, we will want to stay near to the One who loves us. And when we do learn how to live at home with God in every circumstance, everything else seems to fall into place. Every circumstance of life becomes a shared experience with our Companion, the living God. And therefore all that happens to us and within us, from the sublime to the agonizing, all things are manageable and bearable because we are with the One who loves us and has both the capacity and the desire to care for us. Life lived in that presence is good in every way and for all time.

Therefore, the very young and even the very old, held in the strong arms of God, find life good and fulfilling. Contentment, peace, joy, and hope blossom and bear the fruit of confidence, assurance, trust, and service to the world, and that *is* a life fully lived. And the young and the very old, held close in the strong arms of God, face the last great mystery of life with deep peace, hope, and radical trust in the One who has been redeemer, companion, and helper all of their days.

But how do we stay near to God for a lifetime? How do we learn to pay attention to this One whose presence is often unannounced but is always with us? Knowing what we now know, how shall we live? What are the practices and disciplines that can keep us close to the One who loves us in every circumstance of life? What is the way for the very young or the very old to stay in close and abiding relationship with God, to live in faithfulness and obedience to the highest we know? While there is no one specific way that fits everyone, there is a way to find a path unique to each of us and yet common to all. We can find a path that will lead each one of us to a fuller life, a life that really is abundant and really is eternal. It is this pathway that countless numbers have followed in the past and a path that countless numbers follow today. It is a path that each of us can discover, fashion, and follow for ourselves. It is this general path that I will seek to describe and that I invite you to incorporate into your own way of living.

Creating Spiritual Practices

I must remind you that there will be many voices within and without that will seek to lead you in other paths than the one that is right for you and that leads to living fully and dying well. There will be voices that say you are too old to begin now. Or, for those still in their early years, you are too young. And for those still building family and career, these demands can easily drown out the gentle voice of the One who loves you most. Young or old, there will be those voices that will say you are too busy or that adopting a way of living centered on your life in God is not possible in our world.

So we must remember that our culture has a strong voice that often leads to fragmentation and not to integration and wholeness. And while the Christian faith is a wonderful way of life, it is not an easy way of life to practice in our noisy world. The good news is that we have the experience of those who have gone before to teach us, and most of all we have the promised presence of the Holy Spirit to guide and direct us every day and all the way in companionship with God.

Some of those who have gone before spoke of a rule of life, a way of living for every day, for each week, for each month, and for the entire year. Speaking of a way of living rather than a rule of life implies more openness, freedom, and movement than a rule of life. I invite you now to explore what a way of living might look like for those of us who seek to be faithful to God and find ourselves living in the twenty-first century.

We begin by thinking about how we will structure our day so that it will lead us to be more fully alive and more fully aware of and faithful to God. A good place to begin is to select a sacred place and time where we can be completely present with God. This can be early morning, late night or anytime in between. But it is important to find that time and place that is right for you. It should be a time when you can give your whole attention to the One who loves you and seeks your companionship all day long. This sacred space and time will be carefully and prayerfully chosen and finally determined by your own unique personality, needs, and desire to be faithful.

Many find that sacred time in the early morning sets them on a course that guides them throughout the day. Beginning my day by acknowledging and inviting God's presence into my life immediately sets me on a path of companionship that can sustain me all day long. And as I grow in my faithfulness, what begins in the early morning will continue until my eyes close in sleep at the end of the day. Of course, I will have resources to enrich this holy time: the Bible, some other spiritual reading, and perhaps a cross, a flower, or some other object that calls my attention to God as made known in Jesus Christ. Muslims have prescribed prayer five times a day. Some Christians have prescribed prayer seven times a day. Some Christians seek to follow the Biblical admonition to pray without ceasing.

Sometimes, when we are overcome with need or gratitude, our prayers flow easily. At other times we simply desire to rest in God's presence and to be enveloped in God's love and grace. And yet there are times when it is helpful to have some reminders that call us back to awareness of God's presence. The Bible or a cross, a verse of Scripture or a wise saying carefully placed, can remind us who we are and whose we are. Many find that upon arising, during mealtimes, and at bedtime are very natural moments that can call us to pay attention to God's presence and offer our gratitude for God's grace in our lives.

Many find that a special place can help designate this special meeting with God. This special place will also be determined by our circumstances. Remember that every place is made holy and sacred as we invite and acknowledge God's presence. So whether we are living in a single room or a mansion, we can set aside a place for our daily conversation with God. A desk, a kitchen table, a window with a view or special light, a favorite chair, or for those who have more severe limitations, the bed in which we rest, can become that sacred and holy space. This space can become for us the altar from which we feed on the goodness and presence of God and the altar upon which we offer our lives anew to the One who loves us beyond our ability to fully comprehend.

A way of living with God will include much more than can be shared in this brief chapter, but there are a few things that all of us need to include in our path of companionship with God. While we live in a very individualistic culture, the fruits of the Christian faith cannot be fully received apart from community. Being an active part of a community of faith brings spiritual benefit as well as intellectual and emotional support. Corporate worship, study, reflection, and prayer are essential elements in our efforts to live fully and faithfully.

A Healthy, Productive Life

Caring for our bodies and minds is also an important part of our journey toward living fully and dying well. We know that a healthy diet, adequate rest, and exercise appropriate to our health and age can extend the length of our lives and greatly expand their quality. We also know that keeping our minds active and alert adds greatly to our enjoyment of life and can add to our over all well-being.

Jesus said the greatest commandment was to love God with our entire being, and the second was to love our neighbor as we love ourselves (Matthew 22:37-39). Consequently, any serious effort to live a balanced life in Christ will include service to others. For some, retirement years means added time and energy to invest in volunteer service. The needs have never been greater, and the opportunities are numerous to use whatever skills we have to serve others. For some, the limitations of health or means may be such that will not permit service that demands mobility or physical labor. But there is no limit to our prayers, words, or notes of encouragement, and of course a portion of our financial resources, to speed and make possible the work of those whose limitations are less severe than our own.

The writer of Colossians offers a beautiful structure for a way of living for all Christians in every century: "As God's chosen ones, holy and beloved, clothe yourselves with compassion, kindness, humility, meekness, and patience. Bear with one another and, if anyone has a complaint against another, forgive each other; just as the Lord has forgiven you, so you also must forgive. Above all, clothe yourselves with love, which binds everything together in perfect harmony. And let the peace of Christ rule in your hearts...." (Colossians 3:12-15)

Living in the Light

During the second year of our marriage, my wife and I were invited to share a summer holiday with friends in a cabin on an isolated Lake in Canada. Because these friends were generous, we continued to vacation there for nearly forty years. When our first child arrived we carried her there, in her basket and during the last years there had our children's spouses and grandchildren to complete our joy. The setting was isolated with water, woods, sky, and fish, foul, and wild animals to capture our attention every day.

One night, when our children were in their teens, our sons called us out to see the northern lights. It was one of the most dazzling and active displays of energy I have ever seen. The rapidly moving and multicolored light streaked from horizon to horizon. It was impossible to take it all in until our sons told us to lie down on the dock. There, on our backs, we were positioned to see and absorb more fully this magnificent and awesome display. It was an experience that none of us will forget.

As Christians our desire is always to live in the light of God's presence. Therefore, the question for us, young or old, is always, "How will we position ourselves to see and receive the light, life, and presence of God most fully?"

May God grant wisdom, courage, and strength to fashion a way of living that always keeps us in the light of God's presence.

Resources

A Guide to Prayer for All Who Seek God, by Rueben P. Job and Norman Shawchuck (Upper Room, 2003).

Sacred Necessities, by Terry Hershey (Sorin Books, 2005).

A Deepening Love Affair, by Jane Marie Thibault (Upper Room Books 1993).

Additional Contributors

Chapter Two: A Theology of Aging
Dr. John Collett is Senior Pastor of Belmont United Methodist Church in Nashville, Tennessee.

Chapter Three: Our Culture's View of Aging
Dr. Rick Gentzler heads the United Methodist Circle on Aging in Nashville, Tennessee, and has authored several books, including *New Beginnings* DVD (2005), *The Graying of the Church* (2004), *Forty-Sixty: A Study for Mid-Life Adults Who Want to Make a Difference* (2001), and *Designing an Older Adult Ministry* (1999).

Chapter Four: Finding Meaning and Purpose
Martha Hickman, a devoted grandmother and author of a number of short stories, essays, and books on grief, lives in California.
Mozelle Cor is an active member of Belmont United Methodist Church in Nashville, Tennessee. Mozelle was a key leader and advocate in piloting a program at Belmont that led to the creation of this resource.

Chapter Five: Getting It All Together: Making Decisions
Mary O. Boyd, J.D., is a practicing attorney in Nashville, Tennessee.
Charles W. Hewgley recently retired as assistant director of the Commission of Aging and Disability of the State of Tennessee.
David A. Jarvis, M. D., is director of Pulmonary Disease, Critical Care and Sleep Medicine at The Frist Clinic in Nashville, Tennessee.
Bonnie Johnson is a registered nurse who works in the area of wholeness and healing.

This program kit includes everything you need to lead a group through *Living Fully, Dying Well:*

- Leader's guide
- Participant book
- DVD with video segments for each of the eight sessions
- Three booklets for congregation members: *Talking to Your Child about Life and Death, Talking to Your Family about End of Life Issues,* and *Visiting and Supporting Friends Facing Death*

068733585X $69.95

DVD

The *Living Fully, Dying Well* DVD gives the leader help in introducing the topic and starting discussion. Video segments for each session average about ten minutes and include varied presenters, including pastors, physicians, and sociologists. Extend the experience with the additional video interviews of real people sharing their stories. This disk also includes three downloadable, stand-alone study sessions available to bring the whole congregation into the program—two for adults and one for teens. 0687333563 $39.95

Leader Book

This leader guide includes everything you need to confidently lead a study that will affect a lifetime:

- The entire content of the eight-chapter participant's book
- Opening worship liturgy for each session
- Highlights and teaching notes for the opening video segments
- Suggested class session plan
- List of helpful books, web sites, and organizations to support and continue exploration

0687466709 $24.95

Congregational Booklets

Share advice and insight with church members, visitors, and family through these concise booklets on practical topics. Sold in packages of twelve booklets, these offer advice families can use today. The convenient size fits easily into a jacket pocket, envelope, or a Bible.

Talking with Your Child about Life and Death
0687490510   Pkg. of 12 $12.00
Talking with Your Family about End of Life Issues
0687333660   Pkg. of 12 $12.00
Visiting and Supporting Friends Facing Death
0687490618   Pkg. of 12 $12.00